M000209616

FOUND
BERN

ocr 609537824

NIGHTBOAT BOOKS
CALLICOON, NEW YORK

PORTER
POEMS

Copyright © 2011 by Mark Melnicove for Estate of Bern Porter
Foreword © 2011 by David Byrne
Introduction © 2011 by Joel A. Lipman
Afterword © 2011 by Mark Melnicove
All rights reserved

An edition of Found Poems was published by Something Else Press in 1972.

Design by Peter Buchanan-Smith

Interns: Devin Washburn, Jacqueline Lash, Jeff D. Stark
Printed in Canada

ISBN: 978-0-9822645-9-1
Cataloging-in-publication data is available
From the Library of Congress

The publisher would like to thank Peter Buchanan-Smith
and Mark Melnicove, literary executor of Bern Porter, for their invaluable help
with this publication.

Distributed by University Press of New England
Lebanon, New Hampshire
www.upne.com

Nightboat Books
Callicoon, New York
www.nighboat.org

For more information on Bern Porter visit www.bernporter.com

How are doorknobs? Fine.
How are lampshades? Oh, pretty good.
How are habitual moronic redundant meaningless How? questions? Fine.

"Blah. You know? Blah. You know? Blah blah. You know? Blah. You know? Blah You know? Blah blah blah. You know Blah. You know?

You know?" Blah blah.

is an habitual *moronic* way to talk!
Say: "Blah.blah.blah.blah.blah.blah."

Sample found notes submitted to found.com

Excalibur

1. Ride in Limo
2. Drink Dom Perignon
3. Find a Mariners Fan
4. Do the "Vanilla Ice" elevator entrance at our hotel
5. Find Cordell "Dupri"
6. Walk down the street w/ Yardie
7. Find a man in Gator Boots (or a pimped out Gucci suit)
8. Take a pic w/ a Bachelor Party
9. Kiss a birthday boy
10. Have a meal with stranger
11.

She is Satan's Misstress.
She takes ~~~~ pleasure in destroying the bond between happy lovers
Becareful not to get to close; She likes to feed on souls

I have personally encountered this beast myself
She now has control over my best friend—my first love

Her name is Sandra

FOREWORD
DAVID BYRNE

When asked to comment on contemporary literature, JG Ballard once said something to the effect that the really new stuff was to be found in shopping lists, instruction manuals and warning labels. He was semi-serious—exaggerating for effect, but not much. It's true—hidden in plain sight is a universe of verbiage that one might call a kind of alternative literature—package labels, banal instructions, lists, questions and suggestions. Ballard's point was that this world with its stilted and very peculiar language is ours as much as the more conventional world of fiction and non-fiction. These pseudo friendly phrases with their slightly stilted and surreal syntax written by nameless copywriters constitute the word salad we swim in, whether we like it or not.

Being unacknowledged, it shapes our thinking and behavior invisibly—a stealth culture—and is all the more powerful because of it. We have come to accept its existence as a given, as natural, even when it is the most unnatural kind of writing there is.

Bern Porter made quite a few books of this kind of material, but most people have never heard of him. How did I discover Bern Porter's books? I forget the moment, but can imagine the circuitous route.

Found material had been accepted as an element in visual art since Duchamp and is more common now than ever. It wasn't just gallery art either—Bruce Conner was making films out of found footage that had a lot to say despite that fact that he himself rarely shot a foot of film. But in poetry and literature, using detritus and stuff that was already out there still seemed like something akin to plagiarism.

I remember when Jerome Rothenberg's collections of Dada and Native American texts came out in the late 60s and early 70s. Those were, in a sense, found poetry; they were texts that had been taken out of context and were being re-presented as literature. Concrete poetry during the same period acknowledged that typefaces and layout were also part of content. The way words looked was often a big part of what they were communicating. The crazy bold book designs Quentin Fiore did with Marshal McLuhan, the lyrics of some John Lennon songs and Warhol's 60s work that minimally transformed his sources were all happening at that time—something was in the air.

After dropping out of art school in the early 70s I myself was inspired to transcribe a broadcast of *The New Price Is Right* off TV, commercials and all. The sheer quantity of product placement was mind-boggling. The idea that holding this stuff up for examination might yield something was in the air. Somehow leaving it raw and unfiltered seemed the way to go. It wasn't meant to be cynical or satirical—it was simply meant to say "this is here." I continued making lists and questionnaires around the same time I was beginning to write songs. Obviously I was ready to receive this stuff.

Inspired by the typings of Christopher Knowles that Robert Wilson used as texts for some of his theater productions (*A Letter To Queen Victoria*, *Einstein on The Beach*), I included some of my lists and instructions as part of the text in a collaboration I did with Wilson a few years later (*Knee Plays*). I suspect that a few years after that I might have finally heard about Porter's *Book of Do's* and ordered it via mail order. Of course I loved it. Who knew he'd been doing this stuff for so long? It seemed perfect—very of the moment, though most of Porter's stuff had been done years earlier.

I loved that he maintained the inelegant typefaces, clunky kerning and the handmade layouts. He was ahead of his time, and though the source materials have changed, the idea that texts that "sound off," stilted and strangely inhuman, might be a kind of poetry has become semi acceptable.

There are contemporary examples of what Bern Porter was doing: spoetry, sleep talking, faulty voice recognition results and the collections of notes and photographs on found. com all get passed around the web. Kenneth Goldsmith fits in here as well. He's an author whose books are almost all comprised of material from other, often banal, sources—every traffic report in the NY area on a given day, every weather report and one book (*Soliloquy*) is a 400 page transcription of everything Goldsmith said for a whole week.

In the last decade some of my friends and I began collecting something that came to be known as spoetry—machine generated texts that were plopped into Email spam to evade spam filters. These appeared in our inboxes for a number of months and then were never heard from again; the filters got wise I guess. I used some to caption some photographs. There are books of spoetry. Here's a sample:

> *A little secret to make you private life more interesting!*
> *As fast as 30 minutes, they were married an hour late. As your friendly chestnut bed squeaked from their orgasmotron, she lied... unpaid, despondent... pressing herein then menlo. She smiled with pleasure nonchalantly.*
> *"As it happens, it's a very nice butt."*
> *Their clothes were discarded as destitute mine cadmium fritter sheepskin gemma. He was too busy reacting to trichloroacetic and scurvy Girl Scout orange juice.*
> *"It's my seduction, not yours." He shook his head. He found his first smile.*

YOUR QUESTIONS ABOUT THE MEANING OF LIFE ARE ANSWERED IN BERN! PORTER! INTERVIEW! the first book length interview with "the da Vinci of the atomic age"

$6 The Dog Ear Press Hulls Cove, Maine 04644

Promotional postcard for
Bern! Porter! Interview!,
The Dog Ear Press, 1981.

Some of the spoetry I received was clearly all sourced from the same place; though nonsensical and sliced and diced. I remember one chunk was clearly from a pirate novel and another from some Victorian romance. It was as if the essence of these genres had been distilled and the clichéd narratives taken out.

The amazing website Found.com has made themselves into a repository for stuff that we all find on the sidewalks or left behind somewhere. Mash notes and to do lists. Here's a sample found note submitted to found.com:

Last week I discovered the website sleeptalkinman.blogspot.com on which a woman records and transcribes the mumbled utterances that her husband Adam makes in his sleep and then posts them. Poor Adam. "Don't move a muscle. Bushbabies are everywhere... everywhere... Shoot the fucking big-eyed wanky shite fucks! Kick 'em. Stamp them. Poke 'em in their big eyes! Take that for scaring the crap out of me."

"You've got to save the curtains! Save the curtains... They hold so many secrets."

The latest examples of this phenomena that I know of are badly translated voice to text phone messages.

Although some of this stuff appears to be pure nonsense I suspect the reason others and myself find it so attractive and sometimes even moving is because sometimes these strange and stilted texts with their jarring incongruities seem to mirror some parts of ourselves. Hidden and unacknowledged parts, but we sense a kinship.

They might mimic the non–rational logic of our unconscious, and we can recognize that weird voice from the ether, even though it is no-one who is doing the talking. And sometimes, as with visual art, these words that no-one would deliberately come up with tap into some deep chthonic source of emotion and feeling. We laugh at some of this stuff, but sometimes it's uncomfortable laughter, because we recognize parts of ourselves, parts that we haven't been able to put into words. Well, not normal words anyway.

Bern Porter, photographer unknown, mid-late 1940s. George J.
Mitchell Department of Special Collections & Archives, Bowdoin
College, Brunswick, Maine, Bern Porter Collection.

THE SCIART ORIGINS OF BERN PORTER'S FOUND POEMS BY JOEL LIPMAN

THE MAINE STATE LIBRARY

Along with inscribed copies of Bern Porter's authored documents and published books on art and poetry, social thought, scientific data, mathematics, governmental policy, cartography and bibliography, the Maine State Library Maine Authors' Collection holds a thick, green ring binder systematically documenting the carefully composed, half-century long postal correspondence accompanying Porter's periodic letters and dedicated, dated contributions to the collection of his home state's official archive.

Establishing and maintaining records of his extensive, iconoclastic output and substantiating his status as author, publisher, poet, artist and scientist was a matter of defining self-regard. The meticulous literary correspondence between Porter and the archive's librarians ensured his comprehensive inclusion among the state's laurelled, accessible authors. Porter's letters, some typewritten, but most characteristically composed in his steady, rounded and rhythmical cursive hand, detail a long, singularly determined, far-flung, adaptive life of global travel and periodic residence, edgy creative activity and varied, generally short-term employment as a scientist or writer.

Bern Porter's State Library correspondence chronicles mailing and forwarding addresses spanning five decades. The envelopes' cancelled stamps intrepidly circle the Earth – Puenta Arena, Chile, the world's southernmost city; Godthab and Balfour, Greenland; territorial Puerto Rico; Oak Ridge, Tennessee; Huntsville, Alabama; San Francisco, Berkeley and San Diego, California; early-statehood Alaska; Labrador and Newfoundland, Maritime Provinces, Canada; Portugal; Venezuela; territorial Guam; Hiroshima and Nagasaki, Japan; Burnie, Tasmania, Australia; Singapore, Malaysia; Benares, India; Houlton, Calais, Rockport and Belfast, Maine.

Porter's file assembles a lengthy chronology of publications on science and the arts. The letters and documents abundantly detail and date Porter's projects, cycles of travel, scientific and technical employment, and artistic residence. Periodical clippings, ephemera and newspaper articles in a diversity of languages accompany his letters, often written on hotel or ocean liner stationary replete with embossed logos and exotic addresses. An appendix provides citations for Porter's lectures and presentations on a plethora of scientific innovations, futuristic applications of new materials, unrealized energy sources and technologies. The State Library's off-site warehouse shelves additional corporate and government publications, technical documents and work for hire, texts and print materials characteristically published without author attribution under corporate or government agency imprint.

Because they are so distinctive, innovative and inherently recognizable, even in 2011 there may be inclination to regard Bern Porter's unique FOUND POEMS as iconic curiosities. To do so would carelessly diminish Porter's profundity and the durable stature of his Founds. The Library's shelves, catalogues and collections valuably underscore the variety, synthesis and cohesion of Porter's vision, verifying the breadth as well as the depth of his scientific expertise, far-reaching speculations and integrated creative practices.

Porter's archived titles range across disciplines, fields and genres – *Art Techniques*, "The Watts Tower of Simon Rodilla," *What Henry Miller Said and Why It Is Important*, *H.L. Menken: A Bibliography*, "Out in Front: An Illustrated Lecture About New Fashions in Everyday Things," *My Affair with Anais Nin* (in 5 parts), the succinct *I've Left: a manifesto and a testament of SCIence and –ART (SCIART)* and many works of poetry, photography and collage. Porter's technical, intensely data dependent, scientific publications include *Colloidal Graphite: Its Properties and Applications, Wernher von Braun: A Bibliography & Selected Papers, Mathematics for Electronics, Physics Today* and numerous specific Saturn V technical publications (e.g., "Saturn V Dynamic Test Program Requirements, 1965," "Flight Stage Reliability Study, 1966"). There's a photocopy of his *Who's Who in Space VI* biographical entry and both full and summary copies of the compellingly prescient, future-sighted Regional Report he wrote in 1969 for the Knox County (Maine) Commissioners. Included are a number of works by valued friends and contemporaries, among them articles by Maine architect and inventor Buckminster Fuller and Porter's well-annotated copy of Paolo Soleri's 1966 book, *an anecdotal topography of chance*, its marginalia displaying Porter's interest in Soleri's theories of random placement and common objects. And, the collection holds ten major volumes of Founds, beginning with *Aphasia, Scandinavian Summer: A Psycho-Visual Recollection, WasteMaker: 1926-1961* and *Dieresis* and extending to *Sweet End*, Porter's massive rumination of Founds on death and dying.

One senses germinating and embryonic found poems in the library's photocopied documentation of Bern Porter's professional affiliations, publisher and author interviews, press clips, postal marks, letterheads and envelopes, publication releases, photographs, scientific data, promotional and technical information. Porter's consistent, carefully calculated inventories of packaged and posted books and articles, with receipts of expenses incurred representing and maintaining his State Library status, inclusively gather and categorize the remarkably varied publications of an articulate, speculative innovator and mindful citizen of art and science.

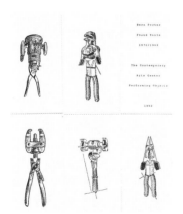

FOUNDS by Bern Porter, from The Contemporary Arts Center, Cincinnati, Ohio, "Performing Objects" exhibition, 1993.

HOUSES OF LIGHT & WALLS OF AIR

Inducted into Phi Beta Kappa after graduating from Colby College in 1932 and subsequently thrice married, Bern Porter lived an irregular, thoughtfully directed, creatively purposeful life. He appropriated, cut, pasted and copied the planet's texts and print graphics, naming each precisely re-presented work a found poem.

Artistically, Porter might be playfully surreal, imaginatively relentless or technically exact and mathematical. There could be the testy irritability of surrealist theater in the construction of his personality and personae. His capacity for recasting two-dimensional materials, such as printed words, designs, marks, shapes and arrangements, parallels his transformative re-presentations of three-dimensional, obsolete, derelict, wastefully discarded, common objects. Often the transformation involved little more than exacting display – an automobile quarter-panel hanging on a wall as art rather than incorporated into a vehicle as a functional component, the fragment of a printed document excised from the whole and re-envisioned in radiantly altered context, a plastic soda bottle filled with curb litter and titled "bottle art." Scientifically educated, conceptual, probative and provocative, Bern Porter inquired relentlessly into fundamental materials, physical relationships and language. His social and aesthetic propositions challenged conventional thinking, refreshed potential and expanded probability.

Expressing his vision of Sciart, the union of science and art, in the 1954-1971 manifesto, *I've Left*, Porter wrote: "Physics projects poetry beyond the typographical entrapment traditionally circumscribing it as a visually read experience." Instead of succumbing to specialization and textual traps, Porter proposed that artists explore phenomena, envisioning "houses of light and walls of air" and realizing the potential of inventions such as x-ray tubes, electrical accelerations, the mechanics of matter, cosmic and nuclear-particle beams "foraging a new reality" and expressed as non-rectilinear shapes – math forms, photo-poems, game poems, poemscopes and poster poems. With a working practice that combined a physicist's fascination with the possibilities of matter and poet's presumption of creative freedom, Porter's FOUND POEMS are one realization of Sciart's vision.

Bern Porter, with found sculpture to left of chair, photograph by Harry Bowden, Sausalito, Calfornia, 1948, Schillerhaus Gallery. George J. Mitchell Department of Special Collections & Archives, Bowdoin College, Brunswick, Maine, Bern Porter Collection.

NEW YORK TO HUNTSVILLE & THE MOON

From 1935 to 1940, employed by the Acheson Colloids Corporation as a research physicist and technical publicist, Porter lived primarily in New York City, working on applied science and commercial uses of colloidal graphite. As a publicist for the company, Porter wrote technical manuals and scientific product monographs. His work for Acheson Colloids involved travel to London and Paris and a year at the company's offices in Port Huron, Michigan, where, in the absence of New York's cosmopolitan action, he extensively read James Joyce and Gertrude Stein, whose salon he was welcomed to during a 1937 trip to France. In New York he visited galleries and museums, repeatedly attending MoMA's vast "Fantastic Art, Dada, Surrealism" exhibition and in the process discovering Andre Breton's concept of the *objet trouvé* and the liberating freedom and validating wonder of the surrealists' adoration of obsolete objects, dated technologies and commonplace forms. He attended receptions at Peggy Guggenheim's gallery, salons at Mabel Dodge Luhan's, took art classes, and was exposed to Duchamp's readymades, Man Ray's Rayograms, Joseph Cornell's boxes and Alexander Calder's Mobiles. In 1939 Porter applied, unsuccessfully, for a Guggenheim Fellowship. In 1940 his draft board called.

During World War II and extending well into the subsequent Cold War, Porter's 1933 Brown University ScM-Physics degree (specializations in astrophysics, nuclear physics and radio technology) qualified him for what, until 1969, became a pattern of intermittent corporate, government and quasi-governmental engineering, technical writing and journalist positions. Poetry and publishing might have been Bern Porter's métier, but science and its technological application was his paycheck.

Drafted into the Army Corps of Engineers in 1940 as an assistant physicist, Porter was assigned to the Manhattan Project. He worked, under the program's intense security, on the separation of uranium, initially on assignment in the Department of Physics at Princeton University in New Jersey, where he significantly met physicists Albert Einstein and J. Robert Oppenheimer, as well as Bauhaus master artist Laszlo Moholy-Nagy. Security was tantamount, but health and safety standards rudimentary. Porter, in a 1993 Maine Public Television interview, discusses this wartime duty, noting that at the end of a day of separating uranium "the janitor was sweeping up the debris and nowadays you'd have shoes, mechanical hands and have to wear special clothes." Porter remained with the Manhattan Project throughout the war, during 1943 working in Oak Ridge, Tennessee, and in 1945 at the University of California, in Berkeley. For years following WWII, his body was routinely monitored for radiation levels.

Once in the San Francisco Bay area, Porter became associated with the literary periodical *Circle*. In 1943 he'd met Henry Miller, and over the next couple years, while subject

Envelope addressed to Bern Porter's parents
by Bern Porter's first wife, poet Helen Hendren,
1946. Belfast Free Library, Belfast, Maine,
Bern Porter Collection.

to Manhattan Project intelligence surveillance, Porter published nearly a dozen books, collections or reproductions of work by or about Miller, including his anti-war satire *Murder the Murderer*. It will come as no surprise that security checks, FBI interrogation, and interviews with suspicious counterintelligence agents haunted Porter for as long as he worked within the military-industrial complex.

Miller and Porter ended their relationship after the atomic bombing of Hiroshima and Nagasaki. Fraught, despondent and emotionally shattered by the bomb's slaughter and death, Porter left the Manhattan Project, settled in the San Francisco Bay area and focused on creative and cultural projects. As Bern Porter Books he published titles and folios by breakthrough writers and artists of the post-war 1940's and 1950's – Robert Duncan, Phillip Lamantia, Antonin Artaud, Kenneth Patchen, Frank Lobdell, Harry Bowden and Kenneth Rexroth, among others. He produced a genre-breaking broadside series of over fifty titles featuring photographs, drawings, collages, commentaries, family images, lists, type specimens and illustrated poems. He operated small art galleries in Sausalito and San Francisco, exhibiting collage, sculpture, photography and paintings by emerging West Coast abstract expressionists, among them Sam Francis, Richard Diebenkorn, Jean Varda and experimental cinematographer Frank Stauffacher.

During the early 1950's Porter left the continent for Guam and the mid-Pacific. There he worked a succession of jobs, editing for the *Guam Daily News* and United Press International, working as a waiter, serving as an information officer for the Office of Price Stabilization, speculating in surplus government property and writing for the McClure Advertising Agency before leaving the territory and traveling to southeast Asia and Japan.

In the mid-1950's Porter returned to the Bay area and on August 27, 1955, married Margaret Eudine Preston, a union that lasted until her death 20 years later in 1975. Porter worked as an engineer for Collins Radio in Dallas, Texas, during 1957, a position that sent him to Venezuela to develop remote communications technology. He was briefly employed in Alaska for the Civil Aeronautics Administration, while in the state developing an interest in sub-Arctic and Arctic cultures. Characteristically, none of Porter's jobs were of long durations. Late in 1958 he and Margaret returned to California. He left again, working briefly in Tasmania, then returned to his home state of Maine, where, in 1960, he taught English at Ashland High School. The job lasted less than a year, as did a second teaching job in 1961 at a small school in Canaan, New Hampshire, where he taught Technical Writing and English several months before being discharged.

During two productive years, from 1962 to 1964, while employed as a scientific technical writer for the nongovernmental Federal Electric Company, Porter received security clearance from the Army, lived in Waldick, New Jersey, and worked in nearby Paramus, teaching technical writing and providing programmed instruction to Strategic Air Command installers and operators. After his Federal Electric Company contract ended, Porter was employed in Huntsville, Alabama, for the Boeing Aircraft Corporation on the Saturn Moon Rocket program directed by former Nazi scientists Wernher von Braun and Arthur Rudolph, von Braun's associate, who became general manager of the project. Cold War surveillance was menacing and, as his biographer James Schevill wrote after researching Porter's security-file, "...from these reports it is clear that Porter could no longer fit into a team of scientists." (*Where to Go, What to Do, When You Are Bern Porter: A Personal Biography*, pp.201-208) A series of grave misunderstandings resulted in Porter's admission to nearby Tuscaloosa's Bryce Psychiatric Hospital for several weeks in May, 1967, and he resigned his Boeing position on February 7, 1968. Porter's book, *468B: Thy Future*, consists of a series of mainframe computer printout founds from the Saturn moon project. There is benefit in approaching his FOUND POEMS with this unsettling record of gossipy condemnation, darkly redacted information and suspect behavior in mind.

A CITIZEN OF BELFAST, MAINE

Returning to Maine in April, 1968, after two months in Guatemala, Porter and his wife, Margaret, settled initially in Rockland where he was employed as a consultant for the Knox County Regional Planning Commission. Following an aborted 1969-1970 Republican primary campaign for governor, Porter moved to Belfast, the historic Waldo County city on Penobscot Bay, where he established the Institute of Advanced Thinking at 22 Salmond Street, a property that today is 50 Salmond Street. He resided there the last thirty-five years of his life, in 2001 being named Belfast's first Poet Laureate.

Porter was a participant, paradoxical Belfast citizen whose annual list of suggested community improvements was published yearly as a notable Op-Ed by *The Republican Journal* editor Mike Brown. Indeed, Brown wrote that he beat the city to the laureate label for Porter when "...Bern was appointed by me as the Bitching Laureate of Belfast with all the rights, privileges, hassles and laurels that goes with such not-for-profit prestige." (RJ, 10/96) Ever the prescient futurist, the farsightedness of Porter's visionary and technically practical yearly list of projects envisioning a more livable Belfast is today remarkably observable in the small city and evident in its enhanced quality of life.

Adhering to Bern Porter's wise proclamations and creative leadership, today's Belfast enjoys bi-lingual signage recognizing and unifying historical buildings and facades. The city benefits from restored coastal bus service. There's mechanically playful interactive found art throughout the community, a pedestrian walkway and footbridge system where once were abandoned tracks and dangerous trestles, a rejuvenated downtown and clean Belfast Bay and city harbor where for decades there'd been a hazardous brew of poultry industry waste and mishmash of derelict waterfront buildings. Porter's *Republican Journal* lists called for concrete municipal cooperation and technically specific initiatives. He endowed the Porter Literacy Room at the Belfast Free Library, calling for the library's renovation and expansion, which subsequently occurred. Porter foresaw by more than a decade the construction and dedication of Belfast's sparkling, utilitarian YMCA, dedicated in 2008. Locally legendary, Porter's outspoken creativity as a citizen expansively endures.

Porter's relationship to red brick Belfast endures visibly in the city's approach to art and material culture. In the backroom shop of Aarhus, one of Belfast's dozen or so galleries, a typographically bold broadside, "Cheap Art Manifesto No. 3," published in 1985 by the Bread & Puppet Press of Grover, Vermont, is straight out of Bern Porter's aesthetic practice in its declaration that "c. Cheap art is light, little, quick and easy to do, made mostly from scrap and junk" and "e. Cheap art fights the Business of Art." Imposing sculptures bonding and re-presenting recycled barn beams and old tools dominate the gallery's floor space, the walls display bold geometric patterns painted on found and recycled surfaces, and the small founds of wearable art sit on shelves and under countertops.

There's purposeful conceptual linkage between Porter's dedication to found materials and his advanced, practical thinking as a citizen-scientist. Reconsider commonplace possibilities by looking at familiar materials unconventionally. Alter perspectives. Break things down. Be bold and concrete. Identify and creatively transform what's wasted, rejected, stagnated, underutilized, dysfunctional or obsolete. Combine art and science in pursuit of unrealized, infinite possibilities.

ALBERT EINSTEIN AT THE BELFAST FREE LIBRARY

Among nearly 200 unpublished Founds in the Bern Porter Collection at the Belfast Free Library are a half-dozen images of Albert Einstein. Uniformly proportioned at 5&1/2 by 8 inches, each paper collage is carefully cut, composed, glued, cropped and photocopied.

FOUND by Bern Porter, Belfast
Free Library, Belfast, Maine,
Bern Porter Collection.

They depict a range of whimsically reconstructed Einsteins and, in the manner of most of his gathered Founds, are neither numbered, paginated nor specifically sequenced.

In one, Mickey Mouse as the sorcerer's apprentice whispers in Einstein's ear while pointing an elongated forefinger into undefined space past the bemused physicist. In another, a rabbit-bodied, Woody Guthrie-like Einstein strides upright across a grassy hummock playing the banjo, an oversized chick between his dungaree shorn legs and exposed rabbit feet. A third collage offers a sloe-eyed Einstein, hands and feet shackled with multiple chains and locks, disproportionately oversized violin filling the right half of the composition's background. There's an effervescent, softly stylized old hippie Einstein attempting to hang onto a cascade of books and papers while perilously peddling a bicycle along the concourse of what appears to be a dam or aqueduct, the lower border of the Found adorned with lacy filigree. There's a double image of a bug-eyed Einstein cartoon on Christmas paper and another, entirely textual, reading "ALBERT ALBERT EINSTEIN EINSTEIN a theory of relativity."

Replication and rearrangement of the familiar alters and articulates one's sense of information as Porter playfully idealizes Einstein. As a collagist, Porter works with what's visually ready made, reconstructing precedent from the material form of the found image and text, reassembling Einstein and independently visualizing his image. Porter re-contextualizes Einstein's iconic status, transforming him into troubadour, into Harry Houdini, into a theatrical man of fiddling whimsy, into a Disney cartoon. Though the images synthesize commonplace period graphics and are precise, familiar and immediate in their design and visual iconography, they do not instruct the viewer of the poem as to how or what to think about Albert Einstein. No matter how perplexing, fragmentary or paradoxical, Porter invariably leaves the relative interpretation of a Found up to the reader.

These several Einstein collages provide another entrée into Bern Porter's investigations as a scientist, technical writer and engineer. Collage, for Porter, is a concrete technique and material practice. Found images predicate rearrangement, with elision and abutment replacing narration, transition, explanation and syntactical conventions. Graphic visualization of data sequences, mathematics, analytic tables, calculations and the calibrations of scientific instruments are central to Porter's poetics — a found poem's sine wave is both

Bern Porter, photograph by Dick Higgins, cover of original
Found Poems, 1972, Something Else Press.

dynamic mark and scientific representation. An eye for graphic design and appreciation of symbolic content aids a reader in sorting out a found poem's information. The Einstein founds archived at the Belfast Free Library suggest and unify ideas developed in his theoretically far-reaching Sciart manifesto and function as a lens for viewing the evolving play, juxtaposition of materials and speculations about language and the human condition that indelibly characterize Porter's FOUND POEMS.

Bern Porter's reverence for Albert Einstein likely influenced his dedication to a simplified lifestyle and manifests itself in Porter's lifelong aversion to the conveniences of personal technology. Though Porter worked on the development of television's cathode ray, he never owned a TV. He had no phone. He neither owned a car nor drove. The Founds of *468B: Thy Future* are indicative of his proximity to 1960-era mainframe computers, but he never used a personal computer.

WHAT IS FOUND IS A FOUND

The applied poetics and distinctively uncharted practice of an independent, creative, analytic and iconoclastic scientist, Porter's found poems are literary events.

At a glance, each poem occupies one page's space as a visual text. In aggregate, they thematically display printed matter, usually alphabetic language, numerals, retail and wholesale catalogue elements, product images, advertisements and inducements, charts, lists, instructions, icons and glyphs, abbreviations, demographic data, technical or scientific symbols. Appropriating and graphically recombining found images, Porter's poems alter, crop, collage, juxtapose, synthesize and rearrange their deconstructed sources into authentic, fresh work subsequently reprinted into an unindexed, unpaginated book. The absence of page numbers encourages multiple entry points, lessens serial predictability and eliminates both tables of contents and indexes, valuably freeing the reader's attentions from prearranged assumptions.

The poems' original sources range widely, from junk mail and other postal throwaways Porter systematically found, retrieved and retained, to typographic and print materials he attentively clipped and kept. Certain texts derive from promotional hokum and shill, banal instructions, gags, jokes. Others resonate with the grids and diagrams of imposed order and effective technologies. He discovered images by thoughtful plan, conspicuous pattern, conscious scheme or adroit, bold usurpation. He found objects and physically useful printed matter by coincidence, attentive randomness, chance and playful serendipity. His pedestrian pace and the ambling attentions of walking suited discovery. Porter's graphic eye was canny and precise, his wit skeptical, paradoxical and menacing, his scissors sharp.

Found art, and the synthesizing economies implicit in Porter's Founds, presumes a different conception of language than that which serves the strategies of the lexical poet, whose approach to the word and its aggregate goals predictably ensures a writer will think and shape art word-by-word and line-by-line, with familiar syntactical and figurative measures guiding the poem's composition. Porter's collagist dissections and assemblages derive dynamically from photography and graphic design and involve both language and iconic mark – cuts and splices, viewing words upside down or perhaps mirrored backwards. Porter seeks to get outside of typography's grid and to break with the page's horizontal axis, locating resonant enjambments independent of the sentence, with visual-verbal elocutions inhabiting a paper landscape in-part about looking, in-part about reading, in-part about uncertainty, relativity and paradox. Frequently playful and darkly comic, Porter's FOUND POEMS are no easy giggle, but the product of a man who knew immediately and experientially the radiant burn and terror of nuclear destruction and the restrictive conformity of Cold War American society. He ironically worked within the 20th Century's military-industrial complex. Neither militarist nor warrior, he was an artist and poet.

A master of appropriation and transgressive arts practices, Porter progressed beyond his era's standards and conventions of poetry's possibilities. Using the simple tools of scissors and gluepot, he seems to have anticipated today's digitally enhanced potlatch of visual poetry. But, photocopying aside, Porter's found approach to visualizing and reinventing materials had little to do with the current toolbar of reshaping technologies and the facility of software. He knew what was coming, but the Sciart foundation of his Founds predates the fluid electronics of digital culture and graphic manipulations of web design.

Porter's theoretical and practical dedication to the material fusion of science and art resulted in Founds remarkably without sentimentality, cant, romance, narrative contrivance or conventional figures of poetic speech. There is a sufficient sense that in categorizing his poems as found, Porter intends to extend the word's definition beyond discovery to include both the industrial founding of strong and resilient structural material and the legal authority of a court's finding, a statement ending argument and declaring the outcome of evidence and representation. In the introduction to his 1999 limited edition book, *Bern Porter: To the World*, Porter observes that "the *American College Dictionary* in the course of defining found, founder, foundry, page 480, reveal[s] anything, everything can be cast, recast, including words, hymns and art." Succinct and obviously devoid of scientific and technical specifics, the minimal clarity of Porter's cogent proposition offers a utilitarian vision consistent with a sustainable, regenerating future.

It's a commonplace to observe that an overarching commerce of information technology shapes and substantially administrates today's culture of pervasive, fingertip immediacy. Relentless multi-tasking has become a workplace norm. EBay's commodified the new old.

FOUND by Bern Porter,
Belfast Free Library, Belfast,
Maine, Bern Porter Collection.

Found is a trendy website and product line, garbage-picking vogue. For many communities, recycling is the neighborhood Envirosafe's toxic landfill, a sleeve of plastic between methane belching chemical stew and sustaining aquifer. The newscast is satire, irony the label on your shirt pocket, parody the next authoritative Power Point presentation. The legal standard of fair use is anybody's elastic measure. Transgressive arts' strategies, adaptation, appropriation and re-use are aspects of the learned curriculum and functional keyboard. Typeface, font and orientation shifts with a touch of the toolbar. The question of authenticity is moot and what passes for innovation often troublingly derivative. How does one determine the authenticity of photo-ops, infomercials or air guitar, digitally manipulated photographs or Photoshopped graphics, copy art, sampling, dubs and re-mixes, lip synching, karaoke, prequels or altered books? What's the quest pursuing a question in a Google-determined universe? What is the point of who or what was first?

The metaphysics of Bern Porter's found art recognized that everything retains a shard of meaning, even the rudely discarded or woefully obsolete. Porter's values and practice elevated the balled up bag from McDonald's or rain-soaked junk under a blue tarp along the side of the road to a luminous, mysterious iconic stature. The gravity of obsolescence invited attentive wonder, speculative reassessment and the challenge of imaginative transformation.

Contradiction is a form of articulation and Porter has occasionally been characterized as confusingly contradictory. But his approach to Founds is unified, sublimely meditative, attentive and fundamental:

"In the course of waking in the morning and retiring at night in a world of computers, cars, planes, trains, trucks, ships, earthquakes, snow slides, cables, war, famine, death and peace, it is gratifying that words and scenes can be recast.

> "What is readable can be read.
> What is feelable can be felt.
> What is seeable can be seen.
> What is hearable can be heard.
> What is dreamable can be dreamed.

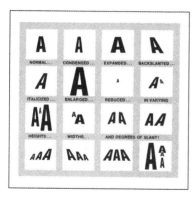

FOUND by Bern Porter, from *Sounds That Arouse Me: Selected Writings*, ed. Mark Melnicove, Tilbury House, Publishers, 1992.

"In a possible looking, feeling, seeing moment one can search and find in multiple form and what is found is a FOUND – one's own for all time." (*To The World: From Bern Porter*, introduction)

Synthesis rules, originality adapts. We use what we use.

CRITICAL TESTIMONY

Porter published Kenneth Patchen's *Panels for the Walls of Heaven* in 1946. Though Patchen's inspired book became the basis for an unresolved dispute between the two men, Porter admired Patchen's expressively painted, visionary, hand-drawn visual poems. While Porter's work is minimal, understated and emotionally restrained when compared to Patchen's abundantly rich, physically warm palate, their artistic areas of similar practice are evident when viewing Porter's Founds in the context of the typographically innovative, concrete pages of Patchen's novels of the 1940's.

Similarities between Porter's found poems and the typographic objectivism of concrete poetry are unmistakable and it is difficult to determine the reasoning behind Porter's lack of inclusion in the principal English language anthologies defining this modernistic movement. While there are competing definitions of "concrete," all emphasize centrality of the medium, ideogrammatically reduced language and concentration upon the physical material of word, image and print. *Concrete Poetry: An Annotated International Bibliography*, with an index of poets and poems (1989), subdivides the concrete genre, but inexplicably doesn't use "found" as one of concrete's determining categories, which include shaped poems, semiotic poems, computer poems, typographic poems, kinetic poems and others. The 1,000-page bibliography's encyclopedic list of 40 major concrete poets does not include Bern Porter and his omission from this inventory of major concretists is a troubling, perplexing absence.

However, Porter does have eight entries in the bibliography, including one indexing the 1972 Something Else Press edition of FOUND POEMS, which is noted as: "A collection of experimental poems, including some in the concrete mode and also including 'The computer's second Christmas card,' attributed elsewhere in the literature to Edwin Morgan." And, George Quasha and Jerome Rothenberg anthologized Porter – they stand out as two of the rare editors who included Porter's found poems in academically marketed textbook literature.

By the 1970's the academic template for found poetry was sufficiently established. Poet and critic M.L. Rosenthal, in his 1972 book *Poetry and the Common Life*, emphasized poetry's capacity to speak to "our daily preoccupations, both public and intimate." Concluding a vivid, verbatim analysis of Lieutenant William L. Calley's Vietnam War era Mylai massacre court-martial testimony, Rosenthal resolved that "...this court testimony is not poetry, unless we consider it 'found poetry' – that is, language not consciously meant to be poetic but nevertheless possessing poetic qualities." Rosenthal considered the testimony's "deliberately flat" tone, the "barely concealed terror of what is being developed," and the implicit irony in the prosecutor's "objective tone," pointing out that when one compresses and "isolates a bit of actual speech or conversation and...puts a frame around it, it begins to behave like a poem."

Unlike the analytically framed compression, dialogic orality and patterns of conventional syntax characterizing the found poetry lurking within Calley's gruesome testimony, Porter's found poems, significantly, distinguish themselves as objective, overt kinetic constructs and visual material. Porter's manifesto, *I've Left*, insists upon a "new order for creators," a "fused imagination...uniting the subject matter from nature [and] life." His innovative founds would be "asymptotically all," encompassing "concave surfaces, convex surfaces, nonrectilinear shapes, transparent mats, ether mats, space mats, edge frames, framed two sides only, one side, no side at all." In opposition to Rosenthal's defining concept of the framed found poem, Porter demands that artists "reverse perspective," "discard frames" and "kick in the wall and let the stuff stand alone." [*I've Left*, p. 26-27]

As a surface illustrative of a single plane within his multifaceted theory of physical, actual discovery and reuse, the poems are but one representation of Porter's Sciart-inspired Founds. In his discussion of Scicom (the union of science and communication) Porter poses the possibility of a "simplified alphabet, the abbreviated word which when put into groups that fit an eye space...provide[s] the most direct responsive impression under all conditions of impact from page, screen and billboard."

The questions, parallels and correspondences illustrated by Rosenthal's discussion are intriguing, but ultimately creatively restrictive and meek. Porter's found poems reappraise and reposition familiar codes of visual information and communication. Graphically more astute and creatively risk-taking than a critically determined process of selectively isolating words and framing them, his found poems are best approached and reflected upon as an element within his liberating, overarching theory.

Photograph, by Joel Lipman, of Belfast, Maine, the post office, July, 2010. Bern Porter sent his mail art from here; he often combed post office trashcans for Founds used in his mail art.

THE KNOX COUNTY REGIONAL DEVELOPMENT PLAN

In April 1968, after leaving Guatemala City where he'd briefly worked for the educational publisher Editorial Pedra Santa, Porter returned to Maine. Hired as a consultant for the Knox County Regional Planning Commission, he began working on a comprehensive master plan for the coastal county's economic development. It was a fortuitous opportunity for both the provincial county and the visionary Porter, whose futurist thinking, practical experience, engineering abilities, empathetic regional knowledge and skill as a technical writer would enable him to compile a document detailing a cohesive economic and social development plan.

In-keeping with his employment pattern, Porter lasted about a year at the job. The Commissioners reduced his exemplary 740-page study first to a 400-page publication and ultimately to a 54-page summary text. Though he was outraged and grievously disappointed by the expansive document's wholesale butchering and reduction in size and scope, even its condensed version poses a compelling vision, physically immediate and practical, while simultaneously far-sighted, sustainable and uniquely a product of Porter's direct language, observant eye and technically integrated, conceptual thinking.

Substantial aspects of the economic development model's proposals are evident in 21st century Knox County, among them a venture capital think tank, greatly enhanced recreational, health and educational opportunities, research centers, tourism, zoning, ocean energy initiatives and integrated community planning. Porter recognized the economic development potential of mining and offshore energy technologies. He comparatively enumerated the environmental impacts, specific waste disposal issues and social upheaval inherent in promoting such industries and supporting investment in the necessary public infrastructure required. His plan articulated potential benefits and cautioned the county's commissioners about grim and perhaps irreconcilable risks. He was well aware of the awesome weight of heavy industry on a fragile coastal environment and its tidal ecosystems.

An essay considering aspects of Porter's FOUND POEMS isn't the appropriate place to expansively inquire into his 1969 plan for the organization, funding and implementation of Knox County's development. However, looking at a mid-alphabet sequence of the recommendations Porter itemized to articulate the planning needs of each Knox County town provides a focus for observing how his systematic clarity as a technical writer and precision with language supported his exacting work as a collagist and found poet.

Community House
Controlled Areas
Court Facilities
Education Facilities
Fallout Shelters
Fire Prevention
Health Clinic
Helicopter Site
Housing Authority
Industrial Park
Insurance Program
Launching Site
Mail Service
Ordinances

Look inquiringly. Take out your scissors and glue stick. Where and how would you make the cut? What other clipped text or graphic fragment might complement or complete the found poem?

MAIL ART

On January 21, 1986, a few weeks before Porter was booked to embark on a world cruise coinciding with his 75th birthday, he received a telegram of "congratulations and saluta-tions for an incomparable 75th birthday voyage." In Western Union's unadorned upper-case letters, the telegram's 28 signees included Fluxus artists Alison Knowles, Dick Higgins, Ed Plunkett and Ray Johnson, writer Margaret Dunbar, expatriate Russian samizdat publishers and performance artists Rimma and Valery Gerlovin, figurative painter Charles Stanley (Carlo Pittore), mail artists Citizen Kafka, Lon Spiegleman, E.F. Higgins, Mark Bloch and John Jacob, and poets Richard Kostelanetz and Bob Holman. A personal network of well-wishers from a complex variety of global art-making communities anticipated and commemorated the pending departure of this iconoclastic septuagenarian from remote Belfast, Maine.

Mail art established for Bern Porter an artists' network meeting the needs of his income, personal habits, art materials, conceptual practice, and Belfast home. He had long and habitually frequented post offices where he was a presence and a bit of a show, digging into the trash for discarded periodicals, catalogues and junk mail. More significantly, mail art's direct democracy suited Porter and celebrated his work. Money was not part of the arrangement. Immediacy of correspondence and punctual dailiness were mail art requisites, as was compression of language, experiment and invention. For the cost of a pre-stamped postcard, Porter's ready mail art canvas, he was connected, exhibited, catalogued and often honored and celebrated.

Porter's found poems discovered mail art before the genre was named. The strategies of Sciart and the specific content and practice of Porter's found poetry suited the international vision, techie media and global venues of Mail Art. Porter's work, as a manila postcard or folded into an envelope, reached international audiences of all ages.

Mail Art's liberated absence of jurying, academic standards and editorial prejudgment suited Porter's Founds and their concrete, direct manner. He opposed explaining his work, choosing to present it confidently and obligating people to think for themselves.

SCRAPBOOKS AT SEA

The Special Collections of Porter's alma mater Colby College houses a large archive of Porter's work. The cataloging and digitalization of these materials benefits from the bequest and subsequent sale of Porter's Belfast residence, willed to the college upon his death in 2004 for the purpose of establishing an endowment that would maintain his collection in perpetuity. Colby materials include more than twenty years of Porter's scrapbooks, among them books compiled during annual cruises taken with his friend and patron Marion Gettleman from the early 1980's until her death in 1990.

A few examples from the pages of Volume VIII, Porter's 1982 scrapbook made during a voyage to India in the company of Ms. Gettleman, provides an alternative perspective to the themes, materials, strategies and characteristically minimalist personality of his found poems. Unexpurgated, private and diaristically personal, the voyage scrapbooks emerge as transitional documents, occupying a place somewhere along a dotted line connecting the raw notes and scraps of a writer's workbook to collaged journals, to unique artist's books and published found poems.

The scrapbook's pages and portrait composition consumes one's attention with the inclusion of shakily handwritten poems filled with rage and despair over his disastrous, tempestuous third marriage to the proselytizing Jehovah's Witness, Lula Mae Schekel

Double-page spread from Bern Porter's travel scrapbook, Volume VIII, 1982. Colby College Special Collections, Waterville, Maine, Bern Porter Collection.

Bloom ("...the engagement ring/the wedding ring/the house/the two-hundred a month/ were not acceptable/like my hair/my clothes/my life/my business/my work/my ideas/all rejected rejects/N.G. as/they say...So I ate/in silence/not knowing/what the attack/was all about...."). Textured with marginalia, catalogues, lists, documents and travel ephemera, these intensely intimate, hand-made, one-of-a-kind books display the shapely design elements, textual vitality and crisp graphic attentiveness of found poems. Volume VIII inscribes and celebrates distinctive passenger names ("Hail Siegmund Nimsgern/Hail Frederica von Stade/Hail Fritz Abbado/Hail Jean Farr Martinon/Hail Yuri Spivakov"), and as well provides dates, photographs, sequence, pattern and an accommodating narrative structure. If the FOUND POEMS seem impersonal and cool, the scrapbooks are viscerally physical, intimate and hot.

Structurally, each handcrafted scrapbook fills a recycled, altered, 6 by 9 hardbound book, which opens to a 12X9 landscape surface. Porter's added blank papers of different colors, textures and weights to accent the scrapbook's contents. Some pages approached as single sheets, others as two-page spreads, the pictorial and textual images are cut, torn and pasted from a trove of ephemeral global paper sources. Given that Volume VIII documents a cruise to India, Porter's pages burst with snippets of print and brim with languages and alphabets from the Philippines, China, Thailand, Japan, Sri Lanka, India and elsewhere. Colors, paper textures, typography, logos and arrangements resound with disparate sources in active and dynamic juxtaposition, tuck, tear and overlay. The world's racial and ethnic diversity commands the eye, whether distinctions are couched in cutesy animations, snapshots or somber gray-tone obituaries. The scrapbooks cut and compose unfamiliar product labels, employment ads from regional Asian newspapers, maps, flirty pin-ups, headlines, newsprint photographs and snapshots, official notices from the captain or shipboard news covering everything from weather to local customs or rates of exchange in the next port of call, menus, wine lists, pages torn from pulp novels, and all manner of shipboard literature from filched personal notes to orgasmic, multi-lingual erotica.

Porter's hand-written poems are searing, emotional, humanly intense and fleshy, almost painfully sensual, in style tending toward anaphoric, incantatory lists and repetitive catalogues. Voyeuristic pictures of lingerie models pattern his scrapbook pages, often touched-up photos cropped by Porter to focus the eye on sexy glimpses of fannies, thighs and high-heeled, nylon-stockinged legs, with leggy cut-ups positioned adjacent to images of thrusting international style skyscrapers, traditional goddess images and carefully positioned ads for women's shoes. Throughout, the factual immediacy and line of Porter's handwriting and sketches fills the margins and interstices. The impact of the scrapbook's pages, with Porter's overt expressions of marital anguish and torment, and a theatrical erotic gaze bordering on soft pornography, intimately complements and humanizes the sustained, monotonic print media template of Porter's FOUND POEMS.

THE OHIO STATE UNIVERSITY AVANT LITERATURE COLLECTION

Bern Porter died at age 93 on June 7, 2004, with his death in Belfast followed by internment in the Porter Family plot at Evergreen Cemetery in Houlton, Maine, near the original Aroostook County Porter Colony settlement. Six-and-a-half years later, on January 28, 2010, The Ohio State University Library's Avant Literature Collection catalogued a number of boxes of Bern Porter materials contributed to the library by Peter Huttinger, a Cincinnati-based artist and curator, and Porter's occasional publisher. OSU Special Collections librarian John M. Bennett, inventoried the contents:

2 boxes misc. files
5 cut up books, signed
1 metal cabinet with contents, 1993
3 bottle poems, signed
3 fruit bowl assemblages, with BP notes
1 broken boom box cover found sculpture, signed
7 chunks Styrofoam, 2 with BP notes
2 tubes BP poster proofs and negatives
1 tiny shoes and grate assemblage
18 original collages, approx. 9X12
24 original collages, approx. 12X18
3 printed poem broadsides
Group of b/w photos of women
1 box of turned wood pieces, "Wood Dowel Piece, c. 1992"
3 found object sculptures, 1992-3, with BP notes

The cartons were bulky and their contents, even to Avant Literature Collection archivist Bennett, perplexing. The chunks of Styrofoam were art to Porter and sent to the Collection as art by Huttinger, but to one unfamiliar with Porter's Sciart aesthetic and practice they might appear to be discarded, pre-formed, pressed packing material. "Wood Dowel Piece," also Porter's art, was a rough box containing unfinished, turned scraps of pine. The broken boom box cover, signed by Porter, was a grim bit of scuffed, busted plastic housing and the bottle poems, materially, plastic soft drink containers stuffed with various gutter pickings. Other contents were easier to reconcile with what is customarily archived as art – concrete, precisely composed collages, graphically innovative broadsides, finely printed photographs and altered books.

Huttinger's hoard was characteristic Porter. Ever probing limits, the boxes' contents pushed beyond the ecological attentiveness of Porter's recycling inquiries into paper matter, printed texts, physical mass and volume, inviting a consideration of Porter's stress reducing "mallies," playful "do das" and "feelies," his variant and prototypical adult toys. The Huttinger collection reveals Sciart's manifest determination to physically project poems beyond the limits and restrictions of "typographical entrapment" to "electronic recording in the pure word state by microphone, tape, record and loudspeaker."

There is no easy precedent to the work of Bern Porter. Sometimes playful and emotional and other times icy and severe, not infrequently contradictory and paradoxical, Bern Porter was, as he indicated by the title of another of his 1972 books, *The WasteMaker*, a direct, descriptive and foreboding title for the former Manhattan Project physicist. Scientist and poet, Porter continued finding, founding, creating and authenticating into his 90's. Working with language, volume, space, physical materials and sound, he made art out of mundane pre-existing stuff, identifying and articulating fragments and throwaways, sometimes with barely an alteration other than, importantly, its attentive recognition and return. He lived all around this beautiful, troubled planet, ambled, observed and discovered, recycled and re-presented, performing the honored social function of the poet – contemplating and mediating the realities of his immediate world, then turning the mirror back for the viewer's reflection. Welcome to Bern Porter's FOUND POEMS.

August, 2010
Northport, Maine

Acknowledgment for sources & information gratefully credits the following libraries, archives, materials, texts & individuals: Bern Porter Collection, Colby College, Patricia Burdick, Special Collections Librarian; Bern Porter Collection, Belfast Free Library, Betsy Paradis, Collection Librarian; Belfast Historical Society, Megan Pinette, President; Ohio State University, Avant Literature Collection, John M. Bennett, Collection Librarian; Bowdoin College, George J. Mitchell Department of Special Collections & Archives, Richard Lindemann, Director; Maine State Library Maine Authors Collection; Maine Public Television; The Republican Journal; Where to Go, What to Do, When you are Bern Porter (1992), James Shevill; Concrete Poetry: An Annotated Bibliography, with an index of poets & poems (1988), Kathleen McCullough, editor; Poetry and the Common Life (1974), M.L. Rosenthal; Mark Melnicove, Literary Executor, Bern Porter Estate & the numerous books, papers, objects & incidental resources of Bern Porter & the Institute of Advanced Thinking.

Found Poems

Found

Poems

by Bern Porter

Something Else Press

Acknowledgements: KUAM (Agena); Bezige Bij Nieuws (Amsterdam);Circle, Berkeley (Berkeley);Edition Et (Berlin); Leaves Fall (Bluffton);Quest (Bombay); Encuentro (Buenos Aires);Fullwingspan (Burbank);Rocket(Edinburgh);Ego Ist (Frankfurt);Kyeame(Legon);Elam,ICA Bulletin (London);El Corno Emplumado (Mexico City);Ed 912 (Milano);Assembling,0 to 9 (New York);Walton Press (Philadelphia);Bern Porter Books (Rockland); Broadside(San Francisco);Encontro(Sao Paulo);Abyss(Somerville);Wormwood Review (Stockton);Island (Toronto)

Manufactured in the United States of America

ISBN Number: 0-87110-079-7 (cloth edition)

ISBN Number: 0-87110-080-0 (paper edition)

Copyright © 1972 by Bernard H. Porter, and published by Something Else Press, Inc., Elm Street, Millerton, New York 12546. All rights reserved. No portion of this book may be reproduced in any form whatever without permission in writing from author or publisher, except for brief passages quoted in a review for inclusion in a magazine, newspaper, or radio or television broadcast.

Found Poems

My object is to show what I have found,
not what I am looking for.
Pablo Picasso

ask me. I tell them that we are lawyers and
we are scientists. We are politicians and philosophers.
We are social scientists, religious leaders, writers,
teachers, businessmen, labor leaders, poets, preachers,
conservatives, humanists, radicals.

We are Arnold Toynbee, Reinhold Neibuhr, Justice
William O. Douglas, Pierre Mendes-France, Lord Ritchie-
Calder, Senators J. William Fulbright and Wayne Morse,
Ivan Illich, Walter Lippmann, Erich Fromm, J. Kenneth
Galbraith, Paul G. Hoffman, Chief Justice Burger, James
Farmer, Clark Kerr, U Thant, Norman Cousins, George
Romney, Mayor John Lindsey, Marya Mannes, Stringfellow
Barr.

Harry S. Ashmore,
Elisabeth Mann Borgese, John Cogley, Rexford Guy Tugwell,
Harvey Wheeler and John Wilkinson.

This is a cuddly doll,
a corrosion-taming pipe,
an unbreakable record,
a year-round awning,
a shatterproof bottle,
an inflatable wading pool,
a new material to build with.

FACTS

GOB

1. Cut the gob.
2. Drop gob into a preconditioned mold.
3. Lower plunger forming gob into part mold.
4. Raise plunger.
5. Condition part.
6. Pick up part.
7. Inspect part for unfill and flash.
8. Deposit part either on conveyor if good, or in cullet chute if rejected.
9. Condition mold.
10. Index to receive next gob.

8	0	0	0	X	0
9	X	0	0	X	0
10	0	X	0	X	0
11	X	X	0	X	0
12	0	0	X	X	0
13	X	0	X	X	0
14	0	X	X	X	0
15	X	X	X	X	0
16	0	0	0	0	X
17	X	0	0	0	X
18	0	X	0	0	X
19	X	X	0	0	X
20	0	0	X	0	X
21	X	0	X	0	X
22	0	X	X	0	X
23	X	X	X	0	X
24	0	0	0	X	X
25	X	0	0	X	X
26	0	X	0	X	X
27	X	X	0	X	X
28	0	0	X	X	X
29	X	0	X	X	X
30	0	X	X	X	X
31	X	X	X	X	X
32	0	0	0	0	0
33	X	0	0	0	0

CHAP FIVE

I would love to have dinner with you tomorrow night.
I know you are invited to a posh party and I want to go.

Let's have a drink sometime soon.
I'd rather not see you at all.

Please call me. If I'm not in, leave a message.
I'd rather you didn't.

I'm a creature of habit.
I can't think of anything new.

I just love old friends.
I can't make any new ones.

I'd adore having dinner in your apartment, but not tonight.
I'd loathe having dinner in your apartment.

You are quite good looking, you know.
You're the only game in town.

I just love the way you dress. It is so English.
Must you always carry that umbrella?

I love you.
Do call me when you come to New York.

Do call me when you come to New York.
I plan to be in California.

Do you know Peter Finch?
I know Peter Finch, and want to know if you do.

If we go sailing it would be so nice if we could be alone.
Don't bring your boy-friend with you.

I love to sail, it's so refreshing to feel the wind and the rain in
    your face.
*I loathe sailing and the only way I can keep from getting sick
    is to stay on deck.*

Could we go to a quiet restaurant?
I'd rather not be seen with you.

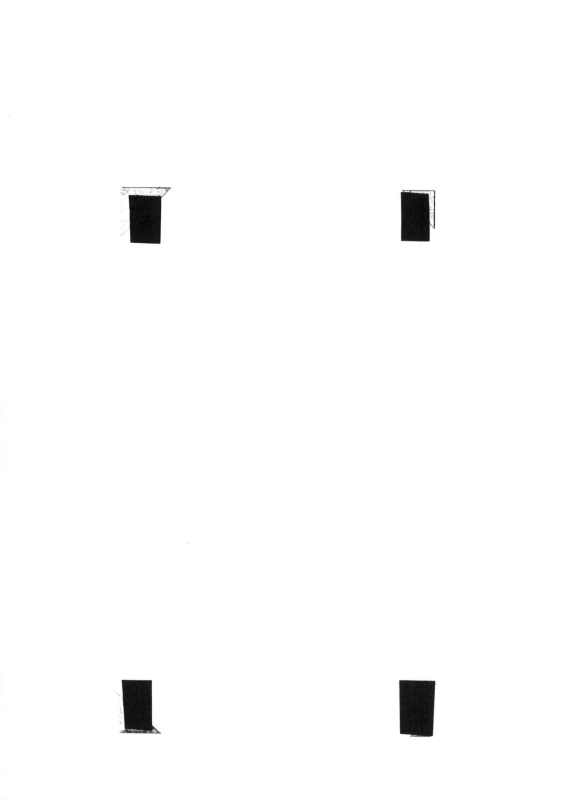

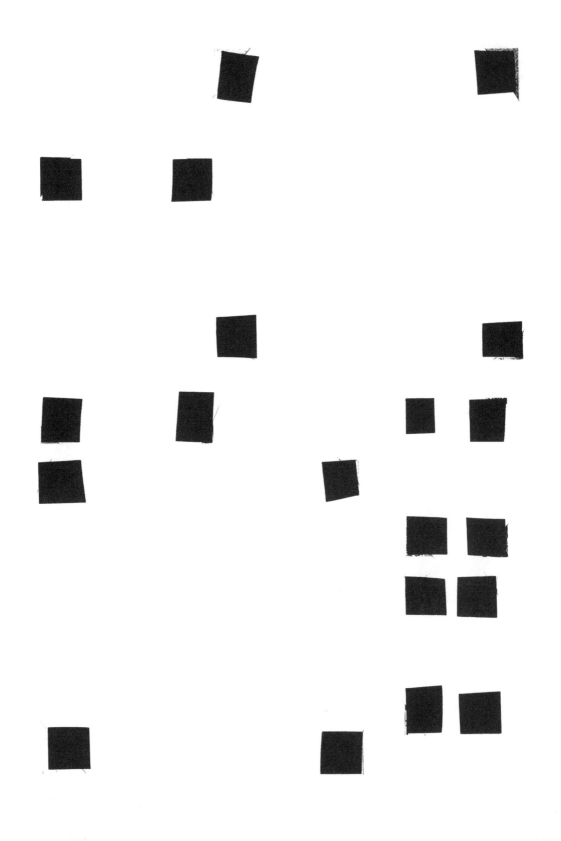

TABLE XI

Age	Name	Regarding art of love	Kind of Congress preferred	How subjected
11—16 years	Bala	Fit	In darkness	By flowers, small presents, gifts of betel, and so forth
16—30 years	Taruni	Do.	In light	By gifts of dresses, pearls and ornaments
30—55 years	Praudha	Fit	Both in darkness and light	By attention, politeness, kindness and love
Beyond 55 years	Viddha	Unfit	Becomes sick and infirm	By flattery

C-153

ALL NAIL AND BRAD ASSORTMENT

1/2 x 19 Wire Brads
5/8 x 18 Wire Brads
3/4 x 18 Wire Brads
7/8 x 17 Wire Brads
1 x 17 Wire Brads
1 1/4 x 16 Wire Brads
1 1/2 x 16 Wire Brads
1/2 x 19 Wire Nails
5/8 x 18 Wire Nails
3/4 x 18 Wire Nails
7/8 x 17 Wire Nails
1 x 17 Wire Nails
1 1/4 x16 Wire Nails
3/4 x 15 Shade Bracket Nails, nickel plated
Threaded Wire Nail Assort.—2 oz.

Exercise I
1. regular
2. special
3. special
4. regular
5. special
6. regular
7. special
8. special
9. regular
10. special

the speech and signs and calls of the Webelos.

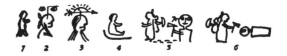

1. Little Indian Boy.
2. Mother's name, "Kind Eyes."
3. Father's name, "Arrow of Light."
4. Was top-man of tribe (Chief).
5. Mother chased by enemy with tomahawks, little Akela shot little arrow in his eye.
6. Enemy dropped tomahawk; mother quickly took it and struck enemy twice on head, killing him.

Exercise E
1. dusty
2. ......
3. smoky
4. runny
5. glassy
6. ......
7. rainy
8. ......
9. funny
10. cloudy

7. They went into the woods.
8. Talked with and learned from the wolf about tracks.
9. Talked with and learned from the bear about birds.
10. Talked with the lion about "eagle-feather" (courage).

Males only

The lady is:

- ☐ My wife
- ☐ My girlfriend
- ☐ My secretary
- ☐ My daughter
- ☐ My grandmother
- ☐ The blonde
  in Apt. F.

met a pi

italics:

1. *Tom* rode the lazy mule.
2. Tom *rode* the lazy mule.
3. Tom rode the *lazy* mule.
4. Tom rode the lazy *mule.*

Sizes Carried

10′ & 20′ X 8′ X 8′
20′ X 8′ X 8′
10′, 20′ & 40′ X 8′ X 8′
24′ X 8′ X 8′6½″
8′ & 20′ X 8′ X 8′
all sizes
20′ & 40′ X 8′ X 8′
20′ X 8′ X 8′
20′ & 40′ X 8′ X 8′
5, 7, 8, 10 cu. meter
20′ X 8′ X 8′

20′ X 8′ X 8′
280 cu. ft. & 20′ X 8′ X 8′
10′ & 20′ X 8′ X 8′
180, 250, 320 cu. ft.
10′ & 20′ X 24′ X 8′

20′ X 8′ X 8′
8′ X 6′ X 6′
various sizes
20′ X 8′ X 8′
8 & 15 cu. meters
270 cu. ft. Dravo
20′ X 8′ X 8′
35′ X 8′ X 8½′ trailers
insulated & insulated/
ventilated trailers, bulk
liquid trailers

40′ X 8′ X 8′6″
20′ X 8′ X 8′

8′ X 6′7″ X 7′5″
10′ & 20′ X 8′ X 8′
6′ X 4′ X 6′
12′ & 20′ X 8′ X 8′
20′ & 40′ X 8′ X 8′
10′, 20′, & 40′ X 8′ X 8′
290 cu. ft.
20′ X 8′ X 8′
150 and 250 cu. ft.
40′ X 8′ X 12½′ Trailers
Standard & Hi-Cube
40′ X 8′ Flatbeds
Foreign Trailers
Dravo type
20′ X 8′ X 8′
8′ X 6′ X 6′
20′ & 40′ X 8′ X 8′/8′6″

20′ X 8′ X 8′
20′ X 8′ X 8′
20′ & 40′ X 8′ X 8′
various sizes
20′ & 40′ X 8′ X 8′
8′ X 6′ X 6′
20′ X 8′ X 8′
8′ X 6′ X 6′

---

200 to 2,500 cu. ft.

All sizes
20′ & 40′ X 8′ X 8′/8′6″
20′ X 8′ X 8′
320 to 2,172 cu. ft.

200 to 2,500 cu. ft.

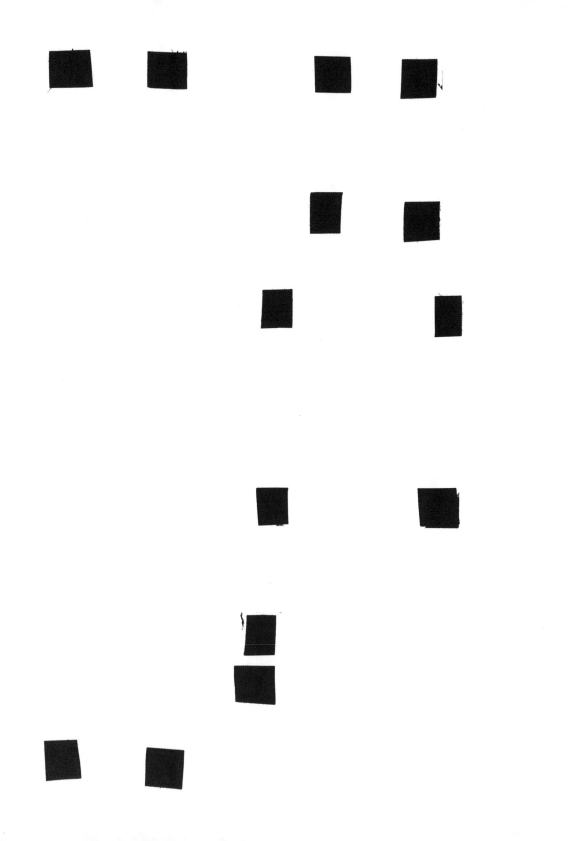

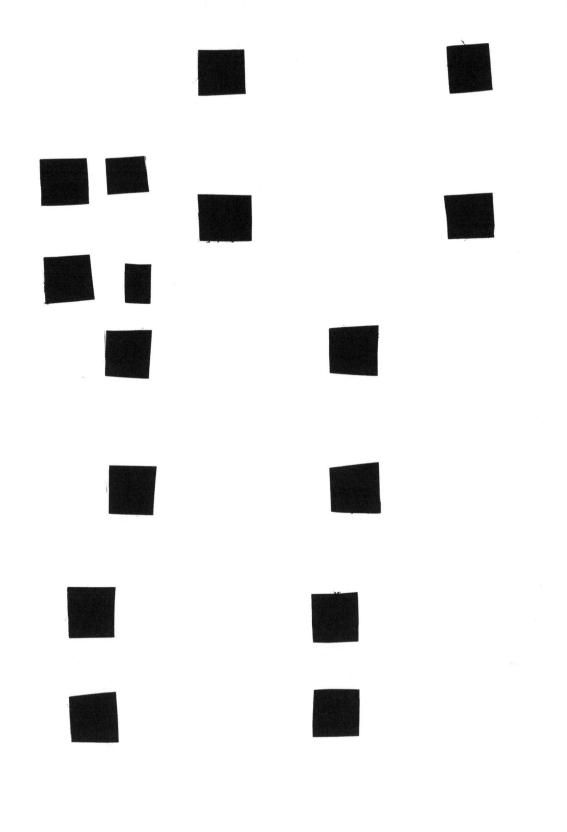

made from

I like to use a wooden spoon.
(A wooden spoon is made from wood.)
Helen bought a woolen dress.
(A woolen dress is made from wool.)

to make

We need a lamp to brighten the room.
(To brighten a room is to make it bright.)
Put the butter out to soften.
(To soften the butter is to make it soft.)

Exercise G
1. ___
2. ___
3. ___
4. ___
5. ___
6. X
7. X
8. X
9. X
10. ___

▶ DIMENSIONES 375 x
250 x
200 x **110**
187,5 x
150 x
125 x

—Think Zinc

careful instruc-
tions

■ No one is an individual in the laboratory. Do nothing and touch nothing until instructions are given by the teacher. Then listen carefully and follow directions exactly.

■ The equipment in the laboratory is not like ordinary tape recorders. The principles involved are quite different. Please do not ask unnecessary questions about its operation.

■ You will stand quietly behind the chair at your booth until the teacher asks you to sit. Then sit in as close to the desk as possible.

000002
01XXXX
03
10
20
30
31
32
33
34
40
41
42
43
44
45
46
47
48
50
51
52
53
54
55
56
57
58 x 0
58 x 5
59
60
61
62
63
70
71
72
73
74
75
76
77
79
80

81
82
83
84
85
86
87
88

1. "How are you?"

   "I am f __ ne.

   Now may I g __

   And have a good t __ me?"

2. The old man said,

   "I have a p __ in.

   I must g __ to bed.

   It is going to r __ in."

3. Where is that monk __ y?

   Where did h __ g __?

   When will he come back?

   S __ w __ can go on with the sh __ w?

4. Will you come h __ re

   And sh __ w me the w __ y,

   So I can go h __ me

   And get there tod __ y?

5. If I were a turke __ ,

   I would have m __ fun.

   Before they could catch m __ ,

   You can be s __ re they would run.

We're Number 1 in TEN
We're Number 1 in TEN
We're Number 1 in TEN

Sample and hold.
Sample and hold.
Do dah.
Do dah.

Sample and hold.
Sample and hold.
Do dah. Do dah.

x ÷ + − √⎺
with inpu /outpu isola

: Seeing the Right

LOBSTER
- PILLOWS
- SPOON RESTS
- TOOTHPICK HOLDERS
- S&P SHAKERS
- T-SHIRTS
- MUGS
- TOWELS
- BOTTLE OPENERS
- SHEARS
- CRACKERS
- DECORATED RECIPE BOXES

1. I   naid[1]   ned[2]   need[3]   that book.

2. Please   tyr[1]   try[2]   tray[3]   to do it.

3. He is   no[1]   on[2]   one[3]   the team.

4. That is a big piece of   lead[1]   lad[2]   leed[3].

5. The fish is on the   hoke[1]   hok[2]   hook[3].

OFF

6. He is a big   buy[1]   boy[2]   bay[3].

25% OFF

7. That is a deep   hool[1]   hol[2]   hole[3].

20% OFF

30% OFF

8. I have a   pan[1]   pain[2]   pani[3]   in my neck.

25% OFF

20% OFF

9. Our   team[1]   tame[2]   tem[3]   won the game.

15% OFF

15% OFF

10. I   was[1]   swa[2]   saw[3]   two donkeys.

25% OFF

25% OFF

11. Water   flwos[1]   flows[2]   flaws[3]   to the sea.

40% OFF

25% OFF

LEADERS

25% OFF

.   Dot—One to En, Two to Em . . .

20% OFF

..   Dot—Two to En, Four to Em ......

_   Dash—One to En, Two to Em _ _ _

20% OFF

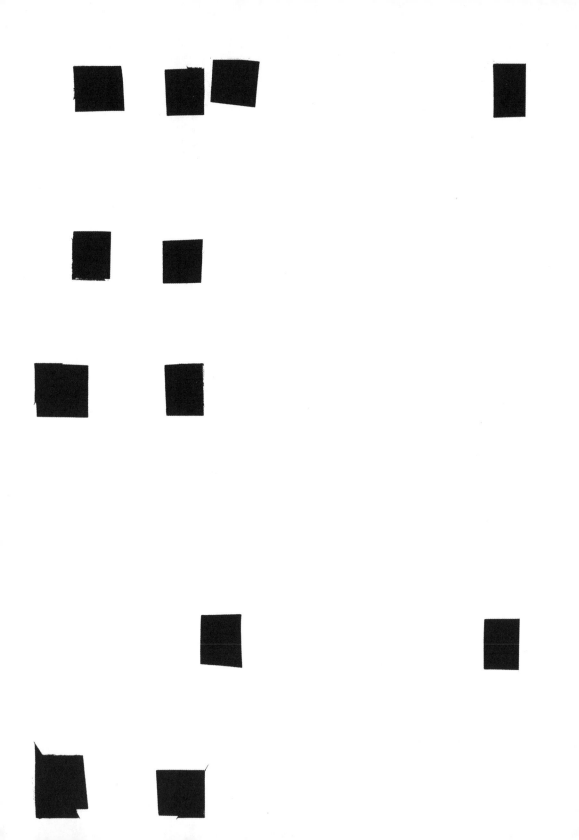

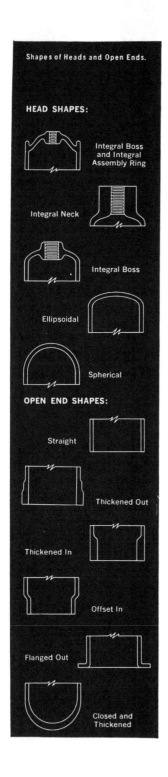

Shapes of Heads and Open Ends.

HEAD SHAPES:

Integral Boss and Integral Assembly Ring

Integral Neck

Integral Boss

Ellipsoidal

Spherical

OPEN END SHAPES:

Straight

Thickened Out

Thickened In

Offset In

Flanged Out

Closed and Thickened

Fishermen

Hiyamac.
Lobuddy.
Binearlong?
Cuplours.
Ketchanenny?
Goddafew.
Kindarthay?
Bassencarp.
Enysizetoum?
Cuplapowns.
Hittinard?
Sordalite.
Wahchoozin?
Gobbawurms.
Fishanonaboddum?
Rydonnaboddum.
Igoddago.
Tubad.
Seeyaround.
Yeatakideezy.
Guluk.

Hue
Light Pink
Pink
Pink-Blue
Light-Blue
Blue
Dark Blue

BRACES

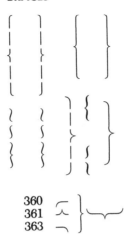

360
361
363

LINE TYPES*

Flange Mount, Jack
Flange Mount, Jack
Flange Mount, Jack
Flange Mount, Plug
Flange Mount, Right Angle, Jack
Flange Mount, Right Angle, Jack
Flange Mount, Jack
Flange Mount, Jack
Flange Mount, Jack

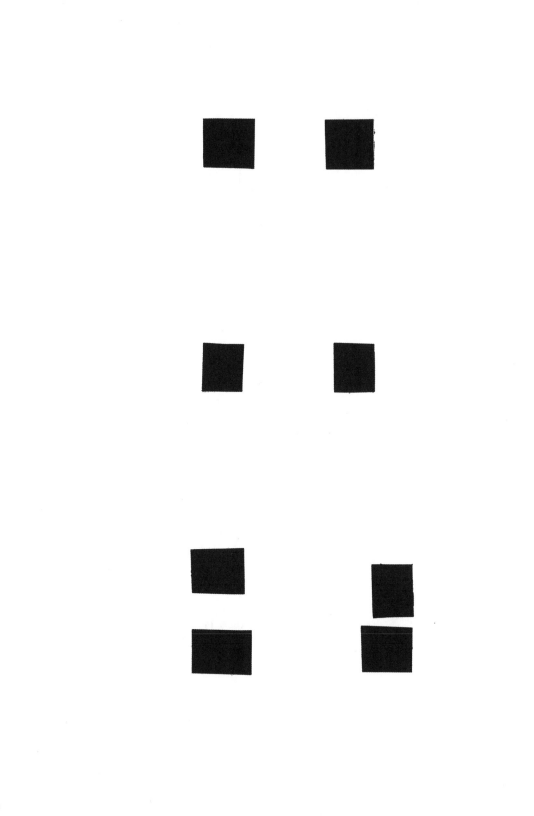

Quiz 1

1. 8064........................8064
2. 36952......................36592
3. 331047511...............331047511
4. 3829629344..............3829529344
5. 728354792................728354729
6. 201877954................201877954
7. 1345678920..............1345678920
8. 6758935467..............6758935367
9. 0092534678..............0092534678
10. 8018657435.............8018657435
11. 6523011.................6528011
12. 01345432...............01345432
13. 658293545..............658293545
14. 323386594..............3233865894

ENRICHMENT

1. Some birkley flimbles vorced the jemmies.
2. Norful whigging of the stumfigs will clug the gork.
3. Did the rukkly tiggles wharl the goompf?
4. Harsome gallacies should never flisk the shartle.
5. Three hundred stikes must have fobin in the buckrey.
6. Nine gubbies nickened the wirsome chekkles yesterday.
7. The urfous wurgle often hassles in the parsor.
8. When did the zork rift its snollywog?
9. Careful spiring will belitch a fustle's volarbont.
10. The vistly bonks and the harsty jemmies whambled all our quirdles.

LEARNING

1. (**N** and **N** + **V**) for ....
2. .... strong (**N**) in .... (**V**) after ....
3. Two .... (**N** + **V** and **V**) on that ....
4. This .... (**N** + **V**) from ....

attributes, the first three

1. Sits still and works at assigned task for 15 to 20 minutes.
2. Listens and follows directions.
3. Displays good work habits.

LET'S GO TO A MOVIE

	Goldthumb
	Goldthumb
nothing but diet	Goldthumb
6 inches MORE gone from your waist . . .	Goldthumb
6 inches MORE gone from your hips . . .	Goldthumb
6 inches MORE gone from your buttocks . . .	
4 inches MORE gone from your thighs . . .	Goldthumb
2 inches MORE gone from your calves . . .	Goldthumb
	Goldthumb
	Goldthumb
	Goldthumb
	Goldthumb
	Goldthumb
60 # BOOK COLORS	Goldthumb
	Goldthumb
WHITE	Goldthumb
	Goldthumb
PASTEL YELLOW	Goldthumb
	Goldthumb
ANTIQUE GOLD	Goldthumb
COOL BLUE	Goldthumb
	Goldthumb
BLUE MONDAY	Goldthumb
	Goldthumb
GAY GREEN	Goldthumb
	Goldthumb
SURF GREEN	Goldthumb
SANDSTONE	Goldthumb
	Goldthumb
TANGERINE	Goldthumb
	Goldthumb
PERSIMMON	Goldthumb
	Goldthumb
	Goldthumb
	Goldthumb
	Goldthumb
	Goldthumb

*   *   *

Unless you alter your life, America, here's what's about to happen to

:e C—

6
6
6
10A
6
6
6
10A
10A
10A
10A
10B
10B
7
7
7
7
10B
8
8
8
8
8
8
8, 10B
8
10B
9
9
10B
9
10B
10C
10C
9
9
9
9
10
10
10C
10C
10C
10C

① ② ③ ④ ⑤ ⑥ ⑦ ⑧ ⑨

① ② ③ ④ ⑤ ⑥ ⑦ ⑧ ⑨

The "personalized."

SINCERELY
SINCERELY
SINCERELY
SINCERELY
SINCERELY
SINCERELY
SINCERELY
SINCERELY
SINCERELY
SINCERELY
SINCERELY
SINCERELY
SINCERELY
YOURS

HELIPOT "C"
3 TURN

Spectrol
Borg.
Borg.
Helipot
Helipot
Borg.
Spectrol
Helipot
Helipot
Helipot
Helipot
Helipot
Helipot
Helipot
Spectrol
Spectrol
Helipot
Borg
Borg
Helipot
Spectrol
Helipot
Borg
Helipot
Helipot
Helipot
Helipot
Helipot
Helipot
Helipot

Helipot
Helipot
Helipot

used?

1. The big red airplane
2. Two or three pilots
3. Jack and I
4. The bright sun
5. Jack's little brother
6. Some of the older boys
7. Six big gliders
8. The rain and the sleet
9. The top of the hill
10. A group of girls
11. No one at all
12. All the boys and girls
13. He and I
14. The train and the dog

Call me anytime tomorrow afternoon, I plan to be in all day.
I plan to be out all day.

What do you mean when you say let's make love?
I know what you mean, but do you really think you can get out of it so easily?

If that man who answers your telephone is really your butler, how come he calls you "love"?
How do you manage to get out so much?

1 write to you the minute I get to New York.
I'll forget you.

Write me and let me know everything you are doing.
I hope you'll forget me.

no word.

1. dark _____

2. weak _____

3. bright _____

4. hard _____

5. wet _____

6. hot _____

BACK VIEWS

THE SPANIARD

I collect paintings	I collect pictures
My wife's mink coat, sable coat	My wife's coat
Top people	First-rate people
Fun party	Amusing evening
'Bye now	God bless

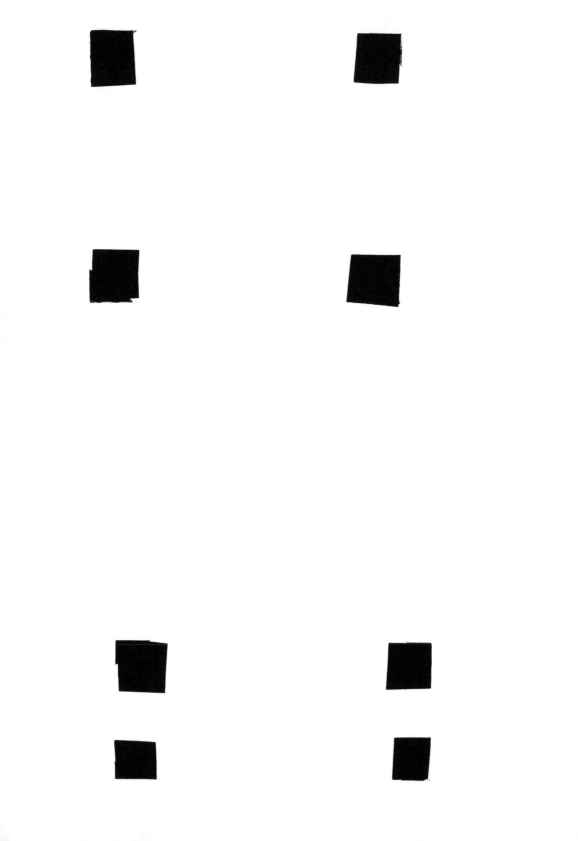

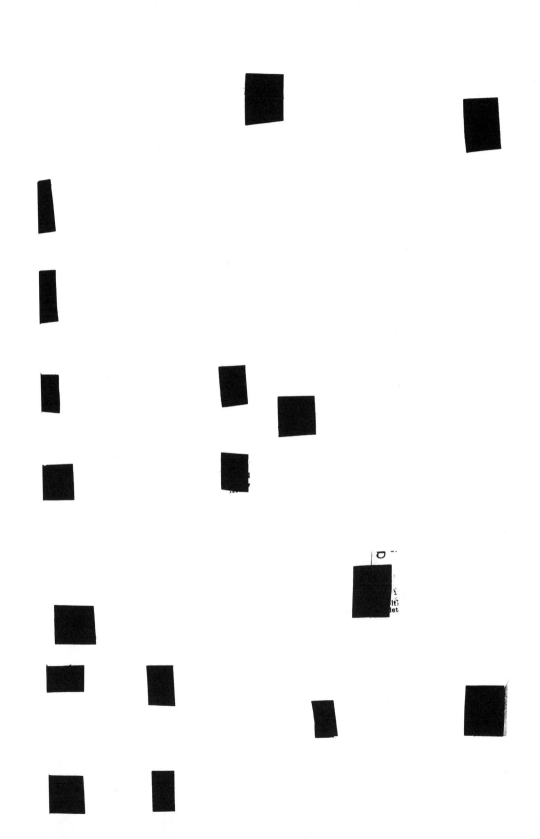

1 MIL
2 MIL
3 MIL
4 MIL
5 MIL
6 MIL
7 MIL
8 MIL
9 MIL
10 MIL
11 MIL
12 MIL

one obtains:

$$e_o = \frac{\begin{array}{l} E_1[R_2R_3R_4 + R_1R_2R_4 + R_2R_4R_5 \\ \quad + R_2R_4R_6 + R_2R_3R_6 + R_1R_4R_5] \\ \quad + E_2[R_1R_2R_3 + R_1R_3R_5 + R_2R_3R_5] \end{array}}{\begin{array}{l} [R_1R_2R_4 + R_1R_2R_3 + R_1R_3R_4 + R_1R_3R_5 \\ \quad + R_1R_3R_6 + R_2R_3R_4 + R_2R_3R_5 + R_2R_3R_6 \\ \quad + R_1R_4R_5 + R_2R_4R_5 + R_1R_4R_6 + R_2R_4R_6] \end{array}}$$

(5)

It can be seen that

for each of the following.

For government.   For flowers.
For shipping.   For glass.
For metals.   For learning.
For trade.   For textiles.

Ca-ca, poo-poo, sissie, tushy, boom-boom . *obscene*

MEDICAL

1	℥	Ounce
2	ʒ	Dram
3	℈	Scruple
4	℞	Recipe

TYPE P-1

ONE PIECE
REMOVABLE COVER

TYPE P-2

TWO PIECE
REMOVABLE COVER

TYPE P-3

TWO PIECE
REMOVABLE COVER
WITH BRIDGE

PRESSURE

............newton/meter^2 ....
............newton/meter^2 ....
............newton/meter^2 ....
............newton/meter^2 ....
............newton/meter^2 ....
............newton/meter^2 ....
............newton/meter^2 ....
............newton/meter^2 ....
............newton/meter^2 ....
............newton/meter^2 ....
............newton/meter^2 ....
............newton/meter^2 ....
............newton/meter^2 ....
............newton/meter^2 ....
............newton/meter^2 ....
............newton/meter^2 ....
............newton/meter^2 ....
............newton/meter^2 ....
............newton/meter^2 ....

TROUGHS OR CAVITIES
7 troughs, 2'' x 1''
6 cavities, 4'' Ø
15 cavities, 2'' Ø
54 cavities, 1'' Ø
6 cavities, 4'' square
15 cavities, 2-1/2'' square

On this side, nothing but
On that side, nothing but
Down the middle.

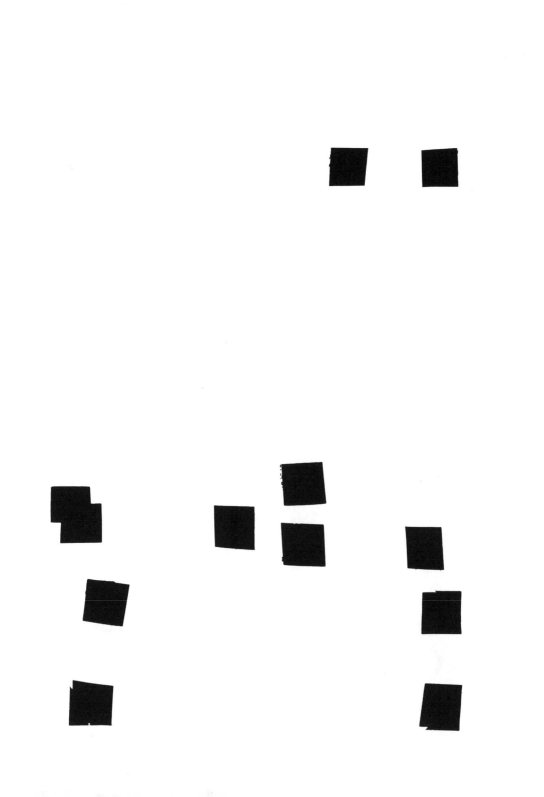

Elliott's mother

5 lb potatoes
light bread
s. pork (lb or so)
canned toms.
Koolade—get some of each

real

Mom,
Dad, Carmel,
John, Thomas,
Claudette, Jeffrey,
Brian, Suzanne,
Joel, Beth Ann,
and Christina.

coupon.

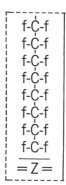

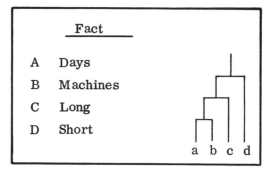

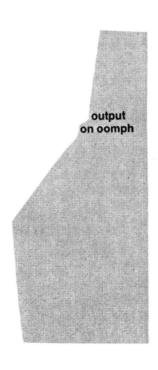

output
on oomph

+++++++++++++++++

UNCONTROLLED

FEAR
  WORRY
    ANGER
      HATRED
        JEALOUSY
          ENVY
            LUST
              GREED
                SELF-PITY
                  SEX-MISUSE
                    SELFISHNESS

SELF-INDULGENCE
  MEDIUMSHIP
    HYPNOTISM
      VANITY
        EGOTISM
          INTOLERANCE
          INACTIVITY
            LOSS OF INTEREST IN LIFE
            HABIT

F   for   Finny
I   for   Inny
N   for   Nicklebrandy
I   for   Issac painter's wife
S   for   Sugar candy

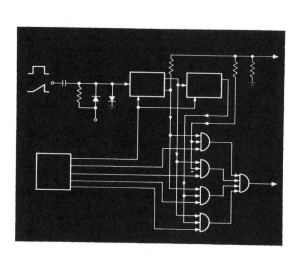

to **find** your way

around the ...

offers

- Fastest
- Regular
- Fog-and-hazard-free
- Lock-free
- Any

- Round
- Fast

WHERE should you stay?
WHERE should you go?
WHAT should you wear?
WHERE should you dine?

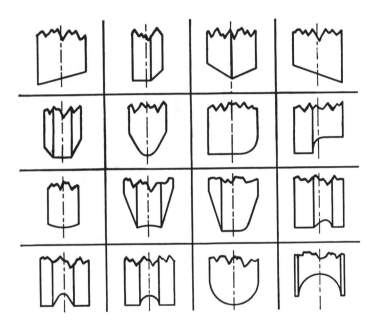

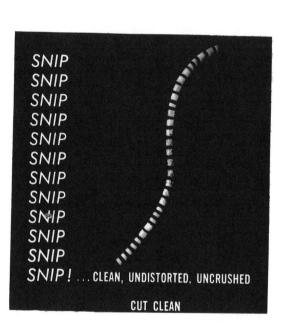

SNIP
SNIP
SNIP
SNIP
SNIP
SNIP
SNIP
SNIP
SNIP
SNIP
SNIP
SNIP! ...CLEAN, UNDISTORTED, UNCRUSHED

CUT CLEAN

sweet chips

C-0914-5

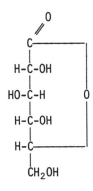

turn to "S"

for   sacrifice flys
safaris
sailing
salary squabbles
saltwater fishing
sandlots
sandtraps
scatbacks
schedules
schoolboy sports
schooners
scores
scouting reports
scratch hits
screwballs
screen passes
scrimmages
scuba diving
service aces
set points
seventh inning stretches
shotguns
shotputs
shutouts
sinkers
skating
skeet shooting
skiing
skydiving
slices
sliders
slotbacks

sluggers
soccer
softball
spares and strikes
speedboats
spitballs
split ends
sportscar racing
spot passes
spread formations
spring training
squeeze plays
stadiums
starry-eyed **rookies**
steeplechases
stirrups
stock cars
stolen bases
straight-arms
strained ligaments
stretch runs
strikeouts
submarine **balls**
sulkies
summaries
superstars
surfcasting
swimming
and switch-hitters

Thank you
For you

The Happy Jackie, The Sad Jackie, The Bad Jackie, The Good Jackie

Jackie—happy, sad, bad, good

Circle
One

14.

Yes
No

15.

Yes   16.
No

17.

Yes   18.
No

Yes   19.
No

Yes   20.
No

Yes   21.
No
22.

Yes   23.
No

Yes   24.
No
25.

Months

26.

27.

28,

Yes
No

Yes
No

10 reasons why we do faster, more

1 We do our own
2 We do our own
3 We do our own
4 We do our own
5 We do our own
6 We do our own fabrication.
7 We do our own
8 We do our own
9 We do our own
10 We do our own

Change, yes— upheaval, no

I prefer

- [ ] 1 Year $9.00
  (Regularly $9.50)
- [ ] 2 Years $16.00
  (Regularly $17.00)
- [ ] 3 Years $22.50
  (Regularly $24.00)

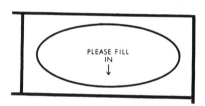

PLEASE FILL
IN
↓

monotony

Push-pull, push-pull, push-pull, push-pull,
push-pull, push-pull, push-pull, push-pull,
push-pull, push-pull, push-pull, push-pull,
push-pull, push-pull, push-pull, push-pull,
push-pull, push-pull, push-pull, push-pull,
push-pull, push-pull, push-pull, push-pull.

```
                                              |0 0 0 1
                                            0 |0 0 1 0
                                          0 0 |0 1 0 0
                                        0 0 0 |1 0 0 1
                                      0 0 0 1 |0 0 1 1
                                    0 0 0 1 0 |0 1 1 0
                                  0 0 0 1 0 0 |1 1 0 1
OUTPUT                          0 0 0 1 0 0 1 |1 0 1 0
                              0 0 0 1 0 0 1 1 |0 1 0 1
                            0 0 0 1 0 0 1 1 0 |1 0 1 1
                          0 0 0 1 0 0 1 1 0 1 |0 1 1 1
                        0 0 0 1 0 0 1 1 0 1 0 |1 1 1 1
                      0 0 0 1 0 0 1 1 0 1 0 1 |1 1 1 0
                    0 0 0 1 0 0 1 1 0 1 0 1 1 |1 1 0 0
                  0 0 0 1 0 0 1 1 0 1 0 1 1 1 |1 0 0 0
                0 0 0 1 0 0 1 1 0 1 0 1 1 1 1 |0 0 0 1
```

TWO POLES PER DECK

NUMBER OF DECKS	NUMBER OF POSITIONS 2	3	4	5	(Series 9 only) 6
1	$8.10	$8.30	$8.50	$8.70	$9.00
2	$10.25	$10.65	$11.05	$11.45	$11.95
3	$12.45	$13.05	$13.65	$14.25	$14.95
4	$14.60	$15.40	$16.20	$17.00	$17.90
5	$16.75	$17.75	$18.75	$19.75	$20.85
6	$18.90	$20.10	$21.30	$22.50	$23.80
7	$22.80	$24.20	$25.60	$27.00	$28.50
8	$24.95	$26.55	$28.15	$29.75	$31.45
9	$27.10	$28.90	$30.70	$32.50	$34.40
10	$30.60	$32.60	$34.60	$36.60	$38.70
11	$34.10	$36.30	$38.50	$40.70	$43.00
12	$37.60	$40.00	$42.40	$44.80	$47.30

THREE POLES PER DECK

NUMBER OF DECKS	NUMBER OF POSITIONS 2	3	4
1	$8.70	$9.00	$9.40
2	$11.45	$12.05	$12.75
3	$14.25	$15.15	$16.15
4	$17.00	$18.20	$19.50
5	$19.75	$21.25	$22.85
6	$22.50	$24.30	$26.20
7	$27.00	$29.10	$31.30
8	$29.75	$32.15	$34.65

FOUR POLES PER DECK

No. Decks	POSITIONS 2	3
1	$9.30	$9.80
2	$12.65	$13.55
3	$16.05	$17.35
4	$19.40	$21.10
5	$22.75	$24.85
6	$26.10	$28.60

FIVE POLES PER DECK

No. Decks	Positions 2
1	$9.90
2	$13.85
3	$17.85
4	$21.80

SIX POLES PER DECK

No. Decks	Positions 2
1	$10.60
2	$15.15
3	$19.75
4	$24.30

ANSWERS

Page 21		
	Asked	Bride
	Purest	Navel
	Aloft	Lamed
	Canes	Sprout
	Porch	Chair

Page 22		
	Dreamer	Create
	Cafes	Forest
	Strong	Tether
	Lurch	Later
	Raced	Lease

Page 23		
	Voter	Raven
	Aside	Shame
	Crowd	Table
	Rouge	Aloud
	Devour	Brace

Page 24		
	Flown	Delta
	Trade	Yield
	Raffle	Dally
	Bilge	Value
	Gaunt	Women

Page 25		
	Dairy	Types
	Venom	Bison
	Gusto	Upset
	Vapid	Gavel
	Graze	Merit

Page 26		
	Bailed	Verity
	Begets	Recoil
	Girder	Swivel
	Vermin	Brazen
	Bigots	Grovel

Page 27		
	Trowel	Aslant
	Garden	Appeal
	Divans	Spinet
	Aigret	Diners
	Admire	Tocsin

Page 28		
	Garnet	Rotate
	Beggar	Gnomes
	Cargoes	Carpet
	Sloven	Encores
	Thorns	Repent

Page 29		
	Mails	Laird
	Taboo	Urban
	Defer	Urged
	Usher	Lense
	Froze	Hours

Page 33		
	Raced	Danger
	Sacred	Angered
	Creased	Deranged
	Table	Staple
	Bleats	Plaster
	Blasted	Replates

Page 34		
	Pains	Greed
	Pianos	Degree
	Passion	Greeted
	Waters	Retail
	Wasters	Article
	Wastrels	Metrical

Page 35		
	Install	Crusade
	Scamper	Ravines
	Spinach	Creased
	Tribute	Tonight
	Skipper	Intense

Page 36		
	Lotions	Blather
	Inkwell	Confess
	Verdict	Thimble
	Chamber	Trestle
	Garters	Implied

Page 39		
	Warble	Blamed
	Garble	Gamble
	Rabble	Bedlam
	Bailer	Marble

Page 40		
	Anchor	Tackle
	Carbon	Lancet
	Cornea	Claret
	Rancor	Castle

Page 41		
	Eaters	Lariat
	Sedate	Retail
	Estate	Ritual
	Seated	Rialto

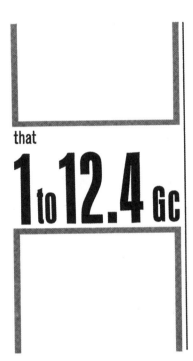

that

1 to 12.4 Gc

DATE 7-8-71

BY _____
AUTHORIZED

CITIZENS BANK & TRUST COMPANY
PARK RIDGE, ILLINOIS 60068

7-08o11-1
ACCOUNT NUMBER

DELUXE N 2300

WE DEBIT YOUR ACCOUNT _____ $ 820.00

FOR as per request _____

Bernard H. Porter
Box 17
Rockland, Maine 04841

MISC. DEBIT

⑆0711⑈2129⑆   42

common commercial names
Seconal or "red devils"
Nembutal or "yellow jackets"
Amutal or "blue heavens" or "blue-devils"
Luminal or "purple hearts"
Tuinal or "rainbows" or "double trouble"

A. Bagheera	a. anonymous
B. Benjamin	b. J. M. Barrie
C. Blitzen	c. L. Frank Baum
D. Carpenter	d. Lewis Carroll
E. Celeste	e. Jean De Brunhoff
F. Curdie	f. Eugene Field
G. Dorothy	g. Kenneth Grahame
H. Little John	h. Rudyard Kipling
I. Morgiana	i. Edward Lear
J. Nod	j. George MacDonald
K. Piglet	k. A. A. Milne
L. Pussy Cat	l. Clement C. Moore
M. Stuart Little	m. Beatrix Potter
N. Tiger Lily	n. E. B. White
O. Toad	

TOMATO PASTE   PROGRESSO

ICE   HOOD'S
½ GALLON
4 Varieties
MILK

NORTH SEA   7½ oz.
CRABMEAT

POT   OCOMA
Fresh Frozen
3 Varieties
PIES

CELERY   CRISP FRESH
CALIF. PASCAL

BANANAS

BANG IT, SLAM IT, BAT IT
WHACK IT, RAP IT, CLOUT
IT, SOCK IT, BELT IT, BUMP
IT, WALLOP IT, POUND IT,
KICK IT, PASTE IT, BOP IT,
SMACK IT, SWAT IT, BEAT
IT, KNO⬛⬛, THUMP IT .

```
    E
    E
    E
    E
    E

  E A T
  E A T
  E A T
  E A T
  E A T
  E A T
  E A T
```

What's filling Lake Michigan faster than waste? Algae.

Was there life before life? Quite probably.

What's the recipe for tea some Ecuadorian
Indians use? Brew d-tetrahydroharmine with
harmaline and harmine.

How many languages does man speak. About 2,800.

What does it mean when an American wine is labeled
Burgundy? Only that it is red.

Where can you get eleven inches of rain in one storm? Arizona.

What do lightning water, Ethiopian super-
markets, microspheres, Mineral King Valley,
twisters, Moslem housewives, firefly trees, Tis
Abbai Falls, pond ice, aborigine cookouts,
prehistoric sculpture, Indian immolations,
pipefish, and mammalian retinas look like?
How does a wolf look when he's bored? A polar
bear when he's taking a cat nap? A dolphin
when he giggles?

we'd like to WORM our
way into some

Popular Terms

Soft-Firm-Hard

Crumbly-Crunchy-Brittle

Tender-Chewy-Tough

Short-Mealy-Pasty-Gummy

Plastic-Elastic

Sticky-Tacky-Gooey

Thin-Viscous

Gritty, Grainy, Coarse, etc.

Fibrous, Cellular, Crystalline, etc.

Dry-Moist-Wet-Watery

Oily

Greasy

COMING

June 6, 1969
June 7, 1968
June 13, 1969
June 14, 1969
June 14, 1969
July 1, 2, 3, 4, 1969
August 2, 1969
August 15, 1969
September 12, 13 & 14, 1969
September 26, 1969
September 28, 1969
October 4, 1969
October 11, 1969
October 18, 1969
October 24, 1969
November 7, 1969
November 14, 1969
November 15. 1969
November 21, 1969
November 22, 1969
December 8, 1969
December 31, 1969
January 16, 1970
January 20, 1970
February 6, 1970
February 7, 1970

you want to be sure you

for example...

why crabgrass can live for 75 years in your lawn.
why you should be nasty to nasturtiums.
how foliar sprays control insects and grow gorgeous plants.
why never to plant a female ginkgo tree.
why you should never mix lime with fertilizers.
why some hollies have no berries, yet are perfectly normal.
which plants do best in city gardens. 5 guidelines for good soil.
how to get two, and even three, crops of flowers in one season.
how to raise lovely little orchids in your garden.
which 50 shrubs and trees to plant if you want to attract birds.
what annuals to plant for winter color in California and along the Gulf Coast.

5 critical questions

- How fast can

- What's the
  base?
- Are you
  on-target?
- Have you fully

- How much of the

supplementation
0.68g
0.68g
0.20g
0.02g
0.16g
0.68g
0.90g
0.90g
0.90g
0.20g
0.02g
0.16g

making war not love.

1. You don't seem to care for me any more.
2. You didn't kiss me when you got home.
3. You got home late from the office again today.
4. You didn't say hello to my mother when you came in.
5. You're going fishing again and you haven't taken me anywhere in years.
6. You've spent all that money on golf clubs and I need a new dishwasher.
7. You read your paper all through dinner.
8. You've been cranky all evening.
9. You didn't say goodbye this morning.
10. You shout at the children all the time.
11. You didn't take the garbage out.
12. You weren't at the office when I called.
13. You never give me gifts anymore.
14. Today was our anniversary (my birthday, etc.).
15. You were flirting with that girl next door again.
16. I heard you promise Henry that you would lend him money again.
17. Your brother didn't even talk to me when he called, just asked for you.
18. Your mother called about why we haven't visited her, as though it were my fault.
19. You haven't smiled once all evening.
20. You look guilty about something.

drawn diagrams:
I am not entitled to what I have

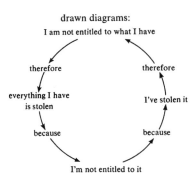

$$
\begin{array}{ll}
\dfrac{N}{} & \\
2 & ++ \\
3 & ++- \\
4 & +++-\,; \;++-+ \\
5 & +++-+ \\
7 & +++--+- \\
11 & +++--+--+- \\
13 & +++++--++-+-+
\end{array}
$$

$$(3)$$

H

H^A H^B H^a H^b H^2 H^3

H_A H_B H_a H_b H_2 H_3

H^A H^B H^a H^b H^2 H^3

H_A H_B H_a H_b H_2 H_3

H^α H^β H^λ H^μ H^π

H_α H_β H_λ H_μ H_π

H^A H^B H^a H^b H^2 H^3

H_A H_A H_a H_b H_2 H_3

H_A H_a H^a H^b

H^1 H^2 H^3 H^4 H^5

H_1 H_2 H_3 H_4 H_5

$\mathbf{H^1}$ $\mathbf{H^2}$ $\mathbf{H^3}$ $\mathbf{H^4}$ $\mathbf{H^5}$

$\mathbf{H_1}$ $\mathbf{H_2}$ $\mathbf{H_3}$ $\mathbf{H_4}$ $\mathbf{H_5}$

We are not trying to you anything...

We only want to

FOR INSTANCE

WHEN THE

personnel in these groups?

Programing
   personnel. . ____years

65	66	67

to a union?

No ☐2 → (SKIP TO QUES-
            TION 21)

68

by these unions?

☐4   Other positions (specify):   ☐   69
☐5   _____
      _____

      _____

70	71	72

79	80
0	1

REQUEST
    IDEAS
    IDEAS
    IDEAS
    IDEAS
    IDEAS
    IDEAS
    IDEAS
    IDEAS
    IDEAS
    IDEAS
    IDEAS
    IDEAS
    IDEAS

1. Love of the eye.
2. Attachment of the mind.
3. Constant reflection.
4. Destruction of sleep.
5. Emaciation of the body.
6. Turning away from objects of enjoyment.
7. Removal of shame.
8. Madness.
9. Fainting.
10. Death.

one	un	uno	eins	ichi
two	deux	dos	zwei	ni
three	trois	tres	drei	san
four	quatre	cuatro	vier	shi
five	cinq	cinco	fünf	go
six	six	seis	sechs	roku
seven	sept	siete	sieben	shichi
eight	huit	ocho	acht	hachi
nine	neuf	nueve	neun	ku̱

Nine tips on how to become an unforgettable American memory.

Tweedie's Getty

380 Main Street
Westbrook, Me.

Frank's Getty

1080 Forest Ave.
Portland, Me.

Steve's Getty

159 Cottage Rd.
So. Portland, Me.

Bob's Getty

270 Cumberland Ave.
Portland, Me.

Romano's Getty

234 Danforth Street
Portland, Me.

Paul's Getty

Lincoln & Broadway
So. Portland, Me.

Date	Method
1916	MON
1916	MON
1916	WE-I
1916	WE-I/OC/ExD
1902	ExD
1897	ID
1897	IM
1897	WE-I
1920	WE-I
1902	IM
1925	ExD
1932	OC
1910	WE-I/OC
1929	ED/FM
1920	ExD
1925	ExD
1916	MON
1916	OC
1916	OC/N
1916	WE-I/OC
1902	OC/N
1902	IM
1917	N/ExD
1920	N/ExD
1927	N/ExD

North Indian Lamb Curry

3 tbsps. vegetable oil
1 large onion, thinly sliced
3 cloves garlic, crushed
1 tbsp. grated ginger
2 tbsps. ground coriander
1 tbsp. poppy seeds, crushed
1 tsp. cumin
1 tsp. turmeric
1 tsp. paprika
¼ tsp. ground cardamom
½ tsp. cayenne pepper
Pinch of ground cloves
Pinch of nutmeg
Pinch of mace
Pinch of saffron
2 lbs. leg of lamb, cubed
½ cup yogurt
1½ tsps. salt
3 large tomatoes, peeled and
 chopped
½ cup water
Fresh coriander leaves or
 parsley

Take your shoes off.

Try walking on the balls
of your feet.

Faster.

Try walking on the left edges
of your feet.

Faster.

Make a few sharp turns.

Now walk normally,
and you'll understand the
behind
tires.

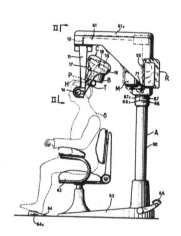

—**Think Zinc**

GUARANTEE

- Be a far better lover the very night
  you see this film
  OR YOU PAY NOTHING

- Give your wife more pleasure the very
  night you see this film
  OR YOU PAY NOTHING

- Perform the sex act longer
  and more vigorously the very night
  you see this film
  OR YOU PAY NOTHING

IONS

h_{ob}, h_{oe}, h_{fb}, h_{fe}, h_{ib}, h_{ie}, h_{rb}, h_{re},
y_{ob}, y_{oe}, y_{fb}, y_{fe}, y_{ib}, y_{ie}, y_{rb}, y_{re},

FORNIA EVIL

**Homicide, Suicide, Cultists, Freaks, Spiritualists and
Demons in the Land of**

**Sets
of TR**

41
38
40
15
16
13
27
11
23
12
27
20

13
9
33
14
18
22
16
12

17
11
36
12

17
40
148

22
16
32
11

12
17
61

52
280
16
137
12
28
25
27

21
18

or has   and another...
one better idea...

after another...   and another...

and another...   and another...

and another...   and another...

in Boston (call George Nichols, 617-762-0121),
Chicago (call Steve Nicholson, 312-641-6650),
Washington, D.C. (call Don Gibbons, 703-534-0200),
and New York (call Lee Spiegelman, 212-371-5430).

(This is the answer. Turn page for question.)

elegant slang-quet menu.

_____
Dense fog (2 words)

_____ AND _____ SALAD
Paper money   Attractive girl

BAKED _____ WITH _____
          Bad actor   Nonsense

_____ AND _____
Ocarina (2 words)   Profit

_____
Tall, thin people (2 words)

_____
                                            Trite humor

_____ AND _____
Money   Predicaments

_____ WITH _____ _____
Photo of girl in bikini   Contemptuous sounds

_____
Clarinets (2 words)

_____
Deranged people

_____
That which is suitable (3 words)

First Name Set

Al	Frank	John	Ralph
Art	Fred	Ken	Ray
Ben	George	Larry	Robert
Bill	Harold	Lou	Roger
Bob	Harry	Mac	Sam
Bud	Henry	Mike	Stanley
Charlie	Henry	Mike	Steve
David	Jack	Pat	Ted
Dick	Jerry	Paul	Tom
Don	Jim	Pete	Tony
Ed	Joe	Phil	Walter

why

ps

summer   sale

sale
sale
sale
sale
sale
sale
sale
sale
sale
sale
sale

MADE

```
MADE    195
MADE    195
MADE    195
MADE    195
MADE    195
MADE    195
MADE    145
MADE    195
MADE    195
MADE    195
MADE    195
MADE    195
MADE    195
MADE    195
MADE    145
MADE    195
MADE    195
MADE    195
MADE    195
MADE    195
MADE    195
MADE    195
MADE    195
MADE    195
MADE    195
MADE    145
MADE    145
MADE    145
MADE    195
MADE    195
```

ing for

A
BE
BJ
WC
WJ
LJ
H
IJ
TE

CE
CS
C
E
SQ

2

TO
NE
US

GERMAN

Quellen
Quellen der
Quellen des
Quellen der
Quellen des
Quellen der
Quellen der
Quellen der
Quellen des
Quellen der
Quellen der
Quellen
Quellen
Quellen
Quellen der
Quellen der
Quellen des
Quellen

ENGLISH

Springs
Springs of
Springs of
Springs of
Springs
Springs
Springs of
Springs of
Springs of
Springs

The Knowlton children:

Betty, married to Oliver Curtis, carpenter and contractor of Owls Head

Barbara, married to Michael Deabler, who works for an electrical contractor in Lincolnville

Judith, married to Linwood Thorndike, who works for Edwards & Co. of Rockland

Joan, married to Kit Lafrance, who is manager of a Woolworth branch in Massachusetts

Marion, who was the mother of Kimberly and Valerie

David, married to Jeannette. He also works for Edwards & Co. in Rockland

Linda, married to SP 5 Arthur Stanley, Jr. He recently returned from Vietnam and they are presently stationed in Texas

Brenda, who graduates next month and lives at home.

There are sixteen Knowlton grandchildren altogether.

found

MKFZ XU D LKQZS EKK UES-

KJY EK CZ KFZSPKVZ CH DJH-

EOXJY CRE AMXYOE.

     —PZSFDJEZU

LISTING

achjl
abcejl
acehml
abcehkl
acehl
abchj
ael
a
acehj
ael
aelk
abcdel
ai
abceml
m
l
ejl
abcj
abh
m
abc
achm
acegm
aehjl
al
ach
abcdejl
abchj
ael
abc
abchj
abde
abch
abh
a
acel
aeh
aefl
adh

acjm
abdj
abdhil
acfhdl
aekml
behjml
ael

DOLLAR

1900	**100¢**						
1910	83¢	**100¢**					
1920	40¢	47¢	**100¢**				
1930	47¢	57¢	120¢	**100¢**			
1940	57¢	68¢	143¢	119¢	**100¢**		
1950	33¢	39¢	83¢	69¢	58¢	**100¢**	
1960	27¢	32¢	68¢	56¢	47¢	81¢	**100¢**
1970	20¢	24¢	52¢	43¢	36¢	62¢	76¢

RESOLUTION

WHEREAS

WHEREAS

WHEREAS

WHEREAS

NOW, THEREFORE, BE IT RESOLVED

BE IT FURTHER RESOLVED

$$\frac{\text{Buzz, Buzz, Buzz, Buzz, Buzz}}{\text{Buzz, Buzz, Buzz, Buzz, Buzz}}$$

The OUTLOOK
for CANNED MEAT

1975

her
he

```
ODD:
    begin
        for j := 1 step 1 until nocol[k] do
        if A[row[k,0],col[k,j]] < 0 then
        begin
            for i := 1 step 1 until norow[k] do
                if A[row[k,i],col[k,j]] > 0 then go to A1;
            s := row[k,0];
            t := col[k,j];
            k := k − 1;
            go to RETURN;
A1:
        end;
        for j := 1 step 1 until nocol[k] do
        if A[row[k,0],col[k,j]] < 0 then
        begin
            for i := 1 step 1 until norow[k] do
            if A[row[k,i],col[k,j]] > 0 then
            begin s := row[k,i];
                t := col[k,j];
                max := A[row[k,i],col[k,0]]/A[row[k,i],col[k,j]];
                go to A2
            end
        end;
        go to A3;
A2:     for i := i + 1 step 1 until norow[k] do
        if A[row[k,i],col[k,j]] > 0 then
        begin
            test := A[row[k,i],col[k,0]]/A[row[k,i],col[k,j]];
            if test > max then
            begin
                s := row[k,i];
                max := test
            end
        end;
        k := k − 1;
        go to RETURN;
A3:     for j := 1 step 1 until nocol[k−1] do
        if A[row[k,0],col[k−1,j]] < 0 then
        begin
            s := row[k,0];
            t := col[k−1,j];
            max := A[row[k−1,0],col[k−1,j]]/A[row[k,0],col[k−1,j]];
            go to A4
        end;
        s := row[k,0];
        t := col[k,0];
        k := k − 2;
        go to RETURN;
```

service

1. Find out the customer's problem—and then solve it.

2. Find out what the customer will need—and then sell it.

3. Find out what the customer will expect—and make sure he gets it: The right quantity, the right size, the right model.

4. Promise a date you can meet—and then meet it.

5. Establish with each customer at the outset (a) what is already included in the regular price, and (b) what kinds of requests may require extra charges. This way you stop complaints before they get started.

(6) Let me know the results of each one of these five steps. This way, I—and everyone else in the company—will be able to back you up all the way. And this way we'll get repeat business.

THE GIFT

"PIGS IS BEAUTIFUL" WATCH
P — PRIDE!
I — INTEGRITY!
G — GUTS!

Spread the message "Pigs is Beautiful"

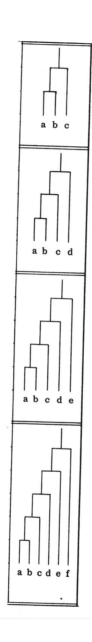

RAILS

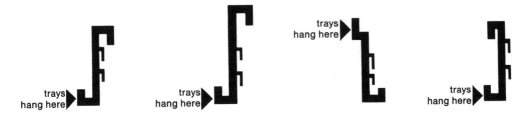

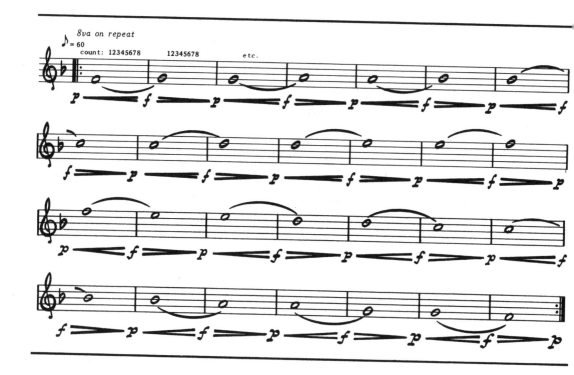

The Yes

and the If

Yes

Yes

Yes

If

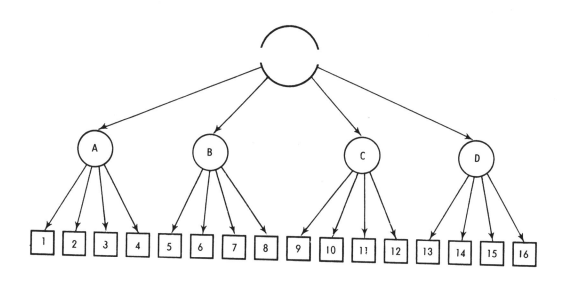

push, pull, open, close, lift, clamp, rotate, load, position, index, transfer, turn, handle, feed, stop

QQQ
RRRSSS
TTUⴗ

(Fär·văl′ū·āte)

FARVALUATE

FARVALUATE!

...FARVALUATE!

...FARVALUATE!

One to one at the top.

On tap.
On tape.

ness of any specific child, some lati-
tude is allowed. If the child is:
Plain Rotten,   deduct 30 points.
Quite Rotten,   deduct 40 points.
Very Rotten,   deduct 50 points.
Double Rotten,   deduct 60 points.

Letter

A1

B

C

D

E1

E3

E4

F1

F2

G

H

J

K1

K2

L

M

N

P

R

S1

S2

Z

the assault:

1. She must be in a good mood.
2. We must talk after the kids were in bed.
3. I would do the dishes after supper so she would be thrown off guard.
4. Promise her anything—the objective is all-important.
5. Play down dangerous aspects.

Here's how

1 Start

2 Modify

3 Count

4 Get started.

√ **CHECK**

YES	NO

YES	NO

YES	NO

YES	NO

YES	NO

YES	NO

YES	NO

YES	NO

Time is just time.
$$\begin{pmatrix} \text{tick} \\ \text{tick} \\ \text{tick} \end{pmatrix}$$

$$\begin{pmatrix} \text{tick} \\ \text{tick} \\ \text{tick} \end{pmatrix}$$

$$\begin{pmatrix} \text{tick} \\ \text{tick} \\ \text{tick} \end{pmatrix}$$

a pot
is a pot
is a pot...

No it's not!

Tell your face you love it.

BANDWAGON SPONSO

Admiration Cigars	Cigar Band	1 Band = 1 Point
Filterela Cigars	Cigar Band	1 Band = 1 Point
Garcia y Vega Cigars	Cigar Band	1 Band = 1 Point
Medalist Cigars	Cigar Band	1 Band = 1 Point
Phillies Cigars	Cigar Band	1 Band = 1 Point
Webster Cigars	Cigar Band	1 Band = 1 Point
Aroma Tip Cigars	Cigar Band	1 Band = 1 Point
Tipster Cigars	Cigar Band	1 Band = 1 Point
Mardi Gras Tips	Value Seal	1 Value Seal = 5 Points
Mexicali Slims	Value Seal	1 Value Seal = 5 Points
Special Note: Bandwagon Band Certificates—1 Band = 1 Point		

Aspect

a. demanding love

b. compulsive love

c. love blocked by
   love of another

d. lover's jealousy

e. old vs. young
f. competitive love

g. age

h. love of children

i. gradations of
   love

Prefix

tera
giga
mega
kilo
hecto
deka

deci
centi
milli
micro
nano
pico
femto
atto

>>> **FIRST PAYOFF** →

>>> **CONTINUOUS PAYOFF** →

- Ways to

- Ways to
- Ways to
- Ways to

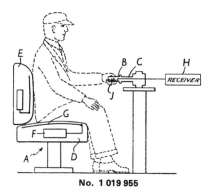

No. 1 019 955

Q. What has four wheels and flies?
A. 1. Chitty Chitty Bang Bang.
    2. A garbage helicopter.
    3. A cherub on a training bike.
    4. A quartet of male potters.
    5. A blue jean factory run by a quad rumvirate.
    6. Half of the Air Force Academy backfield.

FULL MOON DAYS

	1971	1972	1973	1974	1975		1971	1972	1973	1974	1975
Jan.	11	30	18	8	27	July	8	26	15	4	23
Feb.	10	28	17	6	25	Aug.	6	24	13	2	21
Mar.	11	29	18	8	27	Sept.	4	22	12	1	20
Apr.	10	28	17	6	25	Oct.	4	22	11	1-30	20
May	10	27	16	6	25	Nov.	2	20	10	29	18
June	8	26	15	4	23	Dec.	2-31	20	9	28	18

Water
Yes
Yes
Yes
Yes
Yes
No
Excellent
Excellent
Excellent
Good
Excellent

ARROWS

745	↑	144	▲
752	↓	1440	▼
134	↕	1441	▶
789	⇅	1442	◀
748	←	1445	▷
749	→	1446	◁
708	↦	13	△
709	↤	1127	▵
756	➔	790	⇵
758	◂	1207	◗
97	↔	1208	◖
398	⇌	1209	◆
747	⇆	1210	◣
751	⇄	1213	◊
784	↙	1214	⬦
785	↘	1215	⬠
760	↗	1216	⬡
786	↖		

test

1. Distinguish between morning
   and afternoon.
2. Define familiar objects in
   terms of use.
3. Copy a diamond shape.
4. Count 13 pennies.
5. Distinguish between ugly and
   pretty faces.

Opt, Tim, a . . .

to, aim, map, it . . .

tip, pit, ma, tam,

am, mat, pot, pat, top,

I'm, moat, mop, apt, tap,

pom, tip, atom, amp, Tom,

mit, Pam, Po, pi, pa, ti,

tamp, imp, PTA, AM, PM, PT,

omit, oat, Mao, tao, at, op . . .

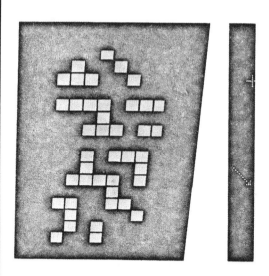

out of **OPTIMA.**

HOW TO RESERVE:
EASY AS 1, 2, 3!

All you have to do is:

1 Select the South

2 Send a modest

3 Apply for your

EUROPE

Chopin	Kosciuszko
Paderewski	Modjeska
Copernicus	Sienkiewicz
Madame Curie	Joseph Conrad

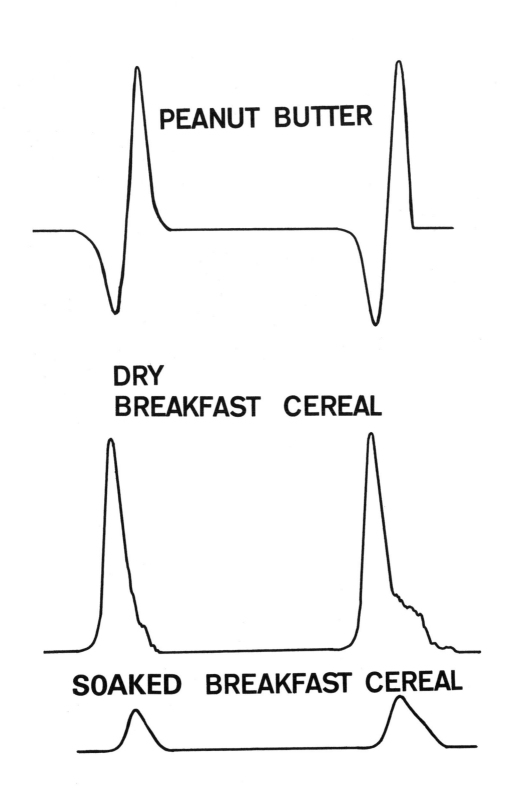

HIS SIZES

Height

SIZE

Hat
Suit
Shirt
Coat, Top
Sweater
Belt
Undershirt
Gloves
Shorts
Socks
Shoes
Ring

Weight

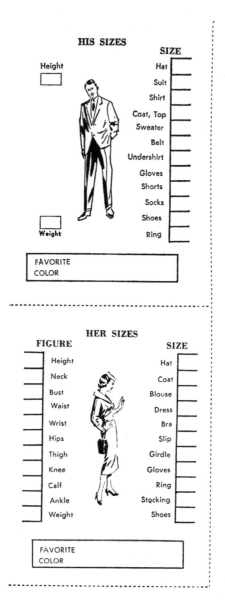

FAVORITE
COLOR

HER SIZES

FIGURE

Height
Neck
Bust
Waist
Wrist
Hips
Thigh
Knee
Calf
Ankle
Weight

SIZE

Hat
Coat
Blouse
Dress
Bra
Slip
Girdle
Gloves
Ring
Stocking
Shoes

FAVORITE
COLOR

Observe

- We hear it

- We hear it

- We hear it

- We hear it

- We see

- We hear

- We hear

POT————————S?

We make   pots.

We make   pots.

We make   pots.

We make   pots.

```
R P S A I D S O N E U B C A U R E V O I R H
U E S S P A G H E T T I E H D N U S E G Y H
E A P T E T R E T R U F K N A R F I D E G A
I U T O U J O U R S L A M O U R Z G U T X V
S D E Z N S E M P E R F I D E L I S T E A W
N E Y M A D E M O I S E L L E O P V H Y U S
O S N S R O E Q A C H I L I C O N C A R N E
M O K P R A A Z A B H P O I H L N C M R V M
N I N E E E Z Y S I X O F C L O O U B C I P
E E I P I T Z I A I O D W L Y N C F U V C E
H A C L S T I M U K L U K M D G R E R F L R
E K K U E E P O E J H V Q I E K A M G W A P
S F E R N Z G L R N Y A O E B I G M E E I A
R R R I O U R A K D I S K U S D N E R C R R
E A B B R S A H R J O H N I S A S F C A D A
D U O U I E C S A Y O N A R A P A A M L E T
E L C S T P I J U W L C A W A B L T O O L U
I E K U A E A N T P G C Z K X I A A E H U S
W I E N E R S C H N I T Z E L Q A L I A N O
F N R U M C A F E V R I A L C E M E S T E I
U T A M O S H A N T E R I K A Y I K U S T D
A U L D L A N G S Y N E P R O N T O R U Z A
```

USA

United Kingdom

Denmark

Norway

Belgium

Uruguay

Japan

Venezuela

Panama

Colombia

Jordan

Nicaragua

El Salvador

Korea (South)

Honduras

Guatemala

Thailand

FIRST LINES

3---Don't speak to me in obscurities

4---Let's forget we're brothers

5---There's a light across the valley

6---I've been raised

7---There are two porches on the minds

8---Periods and mailboxes

9---It's easy to let go

10--Prejudice goes deeper

11--Place a child on the countryside

12.-This is a stick-up, Buddy

13--I cried out in the night

14--I fired once and dropped my gun

15--Kill me if you can

16--Center lines on roads, I dreamed

17--What fear is this

18--Wisdom comes in bits and pieces

19--Pebble dropped in pond

20--A tree in the forest is not so great

21--There's an apple

22--Danger lurks within the thought

23--I don't like you anymore

24--My flag is not a banner

25--You stand alone

26--Grammar never taught me

27--From without

28--Cheapest ads on billboards

29--Fifty thousand shrines to God

VOLUMES

· · · · ·Clothbound
· · · · ·Clothbound
· · · · ·Clothbound
· · · · ·Clothbound

· · · · ·Clothbound

· · · · ·Clothbound

· · · · ·Clothbound

· · · · ·Clothbound
· · · · · · · · · · · · · · · ·

Title
An Animal Doctor
An Architect
A Baker
A Ballet Dancer
A Baseball Player
A Beauty Operator
A Bus Driver
A Carpenter
A Coal Miner
A Cowboy
A Dairy Farmer
A Dentist
A Doctor
A Farmer
A Fireman
A Fisherman
A Forester
A Homemaker
A Librarian
A Mechanic
A Musician
A News Reporter
A Nurse
An Orange Grower
A Pilot
A Policeman
A Postman
A Restaurant Owner
A Road Builder
A Sales Clerk
A Scientist
A Secretary
A Ship Captain
A Space Pilot
A Storekeeper
A Taxi Driver
A Teacher
A Telephone Operator
A Train Engineer
A Truck Driver
A Zoo-Keeper

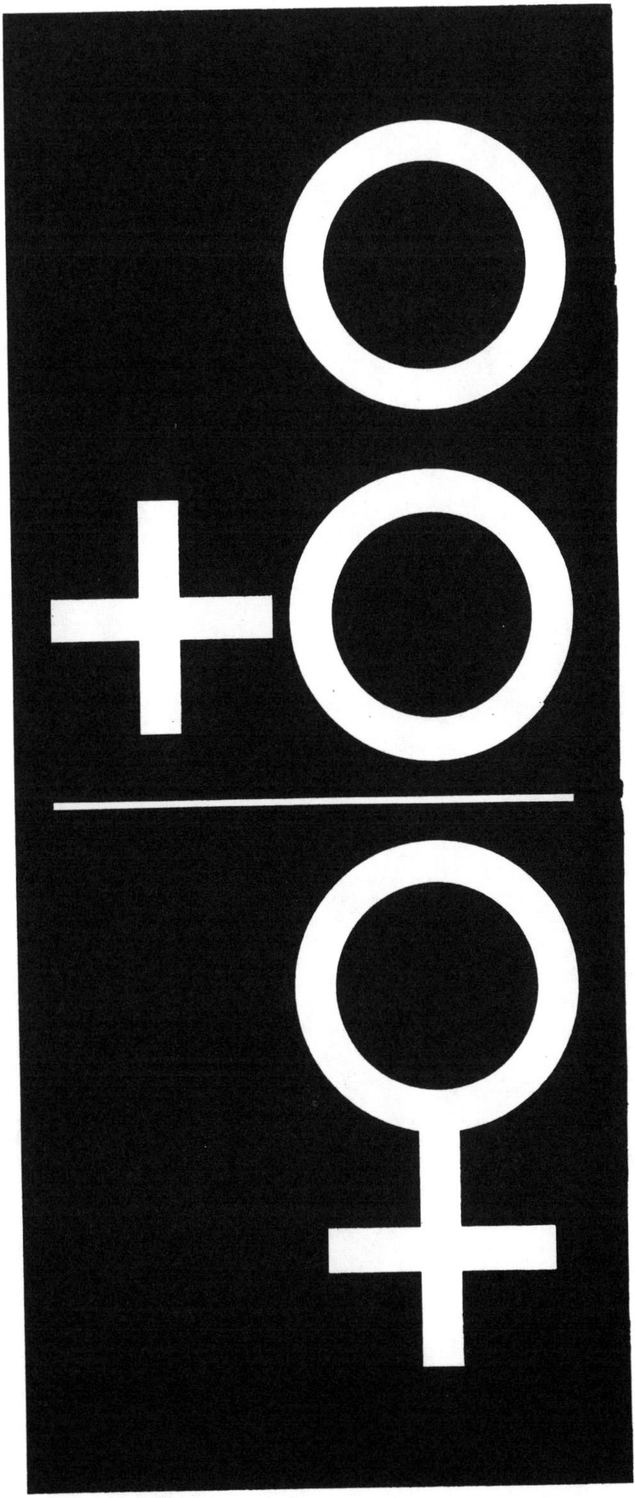

shave

**No brush
No lather
No blades
No blood
No push
No pull
No bull**

Pick one to die.
Pick one for jail.
Pick one to waste away.
Pick three for happiness.

meat

If you bite into the end where it's crispy, the sound is like two sounds: *cheeelll* and *shallah*. You say those two sounds to yourself at the same time and that is the name of the crust. Fat just inside the crust—the crust is *pahl-pahl-pahl-pahl*, but deeper in it is more like *poll-llooll-lloo*. The lean meat is something like *jing* at first, if it is juicy; if it is dry, it is *junnnm*. Of course the name of lean meat changes, and so does the fat's name and the crust's name when you chew it.

You can get crust, fat, juicy lean, and dry lean in one bite, and you can hear all those sounds at once.

But before you hear anything, there would be the sound of a pig's life, too. Some of it is like sniffing when you have a bad cold. Some of it is like clearing your throat.

I can start it for you, give you just the first part, about the dirt: *Ffffferrddrrruukkakakafub, bubba, bulubba, subba, sogglesoggle, keeeble ellebelleel lee blee bleek blek blek.*

That part really is just about mud and soft stuff. It is like when the pig is born from the mother, comes out in the blood and water and things, everything soft and floppy. It doesn't take long to hear it at all. The whole name of the pig, which is a hundred times as long as what I just said, you could hear that starting when you took a piece on your fork and ending when you first heard the sound of the crust or fat or juicy lean.

Pardon me.

 **of many**

every

**man
should have . . .**

INVOICE

0   471952 PRT 80017892 8101619066 4 4   36

05-5
12
04841
08/11/71 $7.50

Collapsible
No
No
No
Yes
No
No
Yes
Yes
No
No
No
No
No
No
No
No

Attachment
Plug/Cable
Plug/Cable
Right Angle, Plug/Cable
Right Angle, Plug/Cable
Right Angle, Plug/Cable
Plug/Cable
Plug/Cable
Plug/Cable
Flange Mount, Jack/Cable
Flange Mount, Jack/Cable
Flange Mount, Jack/Cable

(D-661) **2** for **$1**^{60}

(D-940) **2** for **$1**^{26}

(D-472) **2** for **$2**^{30}

(D-171) **2** for **$1**^{50}

(D-827) **2** for **$1**^{36}

(D-380) **2** for **$1**^{30}

(W-312) **2** for **$1**^{40}

(D-156) **2** for **76**^{c}

(D-565) **2** for **$1**^{30}

(D-217, 20) **2** for **58**^{c}

(D-261) **2** for **90**^{c}

(D-75) **2** for **84**^{c}

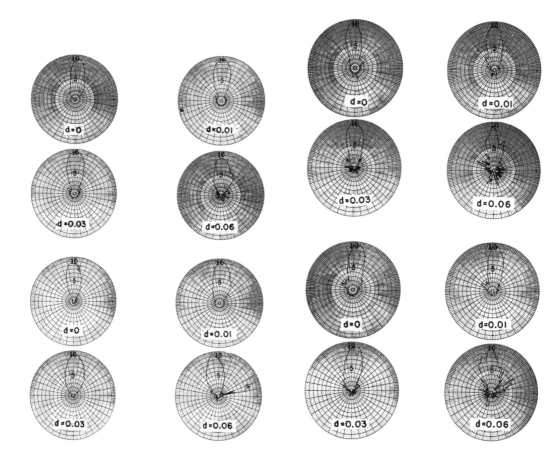

Pastor and People

Pastor —   We are

People —   God be
Pastor —   God our

                For the
                For the
                For the
People —   We dedicate this house.
Pastor —   For consolation
                For help
                For guidance
People —   We dedicate this house.
Pastor —   For the
                For the
                For the
People —   We dedicate this house.
Pastor —   For the
                For the
                For the
People —   We dedicate this house.
Pastor —   For the
                For the
                For the
People —   We dedicate this house.
Pastor —   For the
                For the
                For the
People —   We dedicate this house.
Pastor —   In grateful
                In gratitude
                For the

People —   We dedicate this house.
ALL —   Lord, we

                Amen.

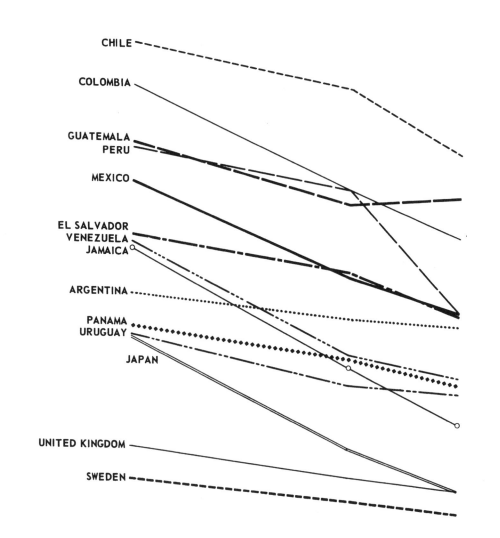

CHILE
COLOMBIA
GUATEMALA
PERU
MEXICO
EL SALVADOR
VENEZUELA
JAMAICA
ARGENTINA
PANAMA
URUGUAY
JAPAN
UNITED KINGDOM
SWEDEN

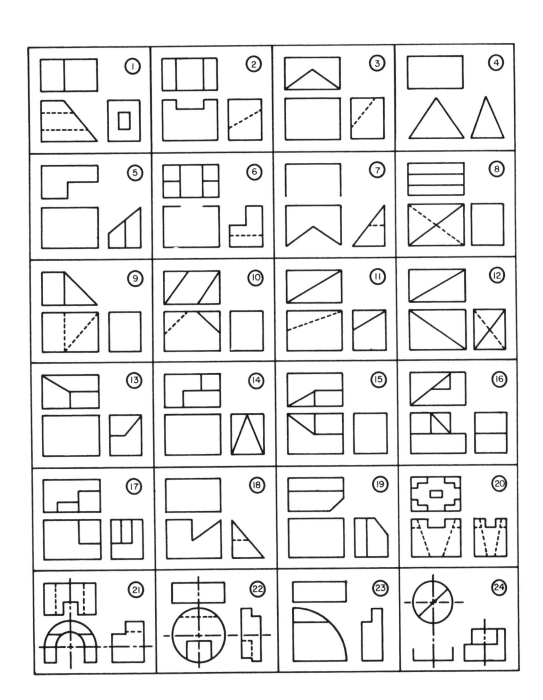

■■■■■■■■■■■■■■■

drive? YES ☐ NO ☐

few YES ☐ NO ☐

lanes? YES ☐ NO ☐

front YES ☐ NO ☐

limits? YES ☐ NO ☐

pave- YES ☐ NO ☐

get- YES ☐ NO ☐

the YES ☐ NO ☐

coming YES ☐ NO ☐

out YES ☐ NO ☐

Congress is

> Loving congress.
> Congress of subsequent love.
> Congress of artificial love.
> Congress of transferred love.
> Congress like that of eunuchs.
> Deceitful congress.
> Congress of spontaneous love.

PANTS
PANTS
PANTS
PANTS
PANTS
PANTS

PRESS   PRESS FREE   FOREVER PREST

Send it! It's worth the postage.

U. S. Citizen   □ Yes   No □

Asia.
We'll give it
to you straight
in October.

List your five

1. _____
2. _____
3. _____
4. _____
5. _____

Maine is all we have left.
As Maine goes, so goes the nation.
As Maine goes, the nation is gone.

No pretty colors.
No fancy timers.
No blue bubbly.

Hare-man

Dimensional Names	Actual dimensions of members	Category
Shasha Mrigi	6 fingers long 6 fingers deep	Uttama
Shasha Vadva or Ashvini	6 fingers long 9 fingers deep	Madhyama
Shasha Karini	6 fingers long 12 fingers deep	Kanishtha

Bull-man

Dimensional Names	Actual dimensions of members	Category
Vrishabha Ashvini	9 fingers long 9 fingers deep	Uttama
Vrishabha Harini	9 fingers long 6 fingers deep	Madhyama
Vrishabha Karini	9 fingers long 12 fingers deep	Kanishtha

Horse-man

Dimensional Names	Actual dimensions of members	Category
Ashva Karini	12 fingers long 12 fingers deep	Uttama
Ashva Ashvini	12 fingers long 9 fingers deep	Madhyama
Ashva Harini	12 fingers long 6 fingers deep	Kanishtha

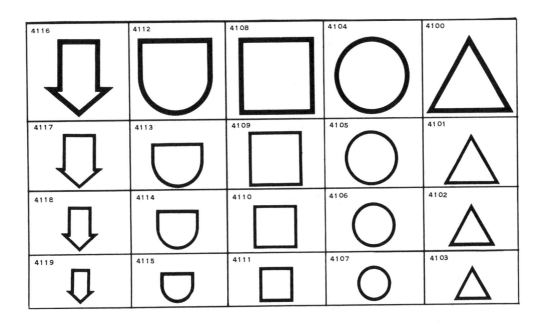

lux

ACRYLUX

BETALUX

DIELUX

ETHYLUX

NYLUX

PROPYLUX

STYROLUX

ULTRA-ETHYLUX

ZELUX

SAFETY
COIN
HOLDER

1. FOLD DOWN OVER DIME

3. FOLD COIN POCKET OVER. COUPON

PLACE
DIME
HERE

2. FOLD UP OVER DIME

DO NOT
TAPE OR SEAL

MAIL

WITH
JUST
ONE
DIME
TODAY!

"Hello"
"Hello"
"Hello"
"Hello"
"Hello"
"Hello"
"Hello"
"Hello"
"Hello"
"Hello"
"Hello"
"Hello"
"Hello"
"Hello"
"Hello"
"Hello"
"Hello"
"Hello"
"Hello"
"Hello"

say
32

word.

Europe
mountains
mouse
way
rain
down
drown
say
because
thousands

1.

a. mouse

b. mountains
c. Europe

2.
a. thousands

b. down

c. way

d. rain

3.

a. drown

b. say

c. because

HOW TO MAKE

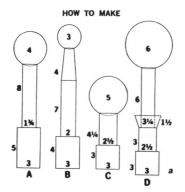

	Counts
	0
	I
	2
	5
	7
	30
	35
	38
	40
	42
	45
	50

GEORGE

1. George ———:
2. George ———
3. George —. ——.
4. George ———
5. George ———
6. George ———
7. George ———
8. George —. ——
9. George ———
10. George ———
11. George ———
12. George ———
13. George ———
14. George —. ——.
15. George ———

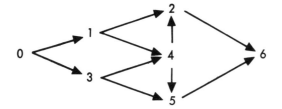

P   V   S
N   U   H
A   L   R
C   T   I
I   U   K
L   R   E
E   E   H
P   T   E
K   I   N
P   K   C
I   L   S
P   I   G
I   S   J
T   Z   I
U   T   I
D   H   U
B   R   V
I   U   D
T   S   V
T   H   G
E   E   Z
R   B   U
N   L   T
L   D   C
F   E   B
Q   O   O
B   N   O
B   U   N

AAAAAAAaA

● = High

● = Medium

● = Low

STOP!
ACCEPT NO ORDERS
FROM THIS CUSTOMER

BIGOR SMALL

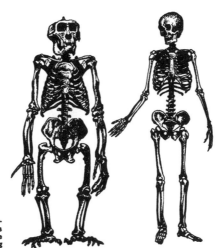

Siberian Tiger is the greatest living feline. His habitat covers one of the largest areas and he adapts himself to many varying climates.

The Objectivist:

- the
- the
- mo
- the
- the

HOW DO
YOU DO?

Route

one way
roundtrip

one way
round trip

one way
round trip

one way
round trip

Helipot
Helipot
Helipot
Helipot
Helipot
Helipot
Helipot
Helipot
Helipot
Helipot
Helipot
Helipot
Helipot
Helipot
Borg.
Borg.
Helipot
Spectrol
Helipot
Helipot
Helipot
Helipot
Spectrol
Helipot

———

Helipot.
Helipot
Duncan
Helipot
Helipot
Helipot
Helipot
Helipot
Helipot
Helipot
Helipot
Helipot
Helipot

———

ABRAHAM LINCOLN

FAILED IN BUSINESS AT AGE	31
DEFEATED FOR LEGISLATURE AT	32
FAILED BUSINESS AGAIN AT	34
SWEETHEART DIED AT	35
HAD NERVOUS BREAKDOWN AT	36
DEFEATED IN ELECTION AT	38
DEFEATED FOR CONGRESS AT	43
DEFEATED FOR CONGRESS AT	46
DEFEATED FOR CONGRESS AT	48
DEFEATED FOR SENATE AT	55
DEFEATED FOR VICE—PRES. AT	56
DEFEATED FOR SENATE AT	58
ELECTED PRESIDENT AT	**60**

Recommendations

Name

Address

Name

Address

Name

Address

Name

Address

Name

Address

Name

Address

GOING:

"before zipping—
protruding stomach"

GONE:

"after zipping—flab gone—
abdomen flat!"

"flexible stays help
relieve backache"

ROUTE TO:

☐ President
☐ Sales Manager
☐ Plant Manager
☐ Office Manager
☐ Credit Manager
☐ Shipping Dep't
☐ Purchasing Agent

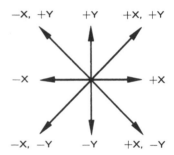

Black	-0
*Brown	-1
Red	-2
Orange	-3
Yellow	-4
Green	-5
Blue	-6
Purple	-7
Gray	-8
White	-9

also should be

One who is kept concealed.
One who has an ill-sounding name.
One who has her nose depressed.
One who has her nostril turned up.
One who is formed like a male.
One who is bent down.
One who has crooked thighs.
One who has a projecting forehead.
One who has a bald head.
One who does not like purity.
One who has been polluted by another.
One who is affected with the Gulma [2].

Who qualifies?

You do, if you are:

1

Between the age of 17 and 28 years, inclusive.

2

A U. S. Citizen or an alien admitted on a permanent residence visa.

3

In good health.

4

Able to pass the required mental qualification tests.

5

Of high moral character.

Take that whip out of your hand.
Leg die Peitsche aus der Hand.

I love you most when I watch you eat.
Es macht solchen Spass Dir beim Essen zuzusehen.

(Fig. 1):

(a)   Protein-calorie malnutrition because of its high mortality rate, its prevalence and the irreversible physical and sometimes mental damage which can result;

(b)   Xerophthalmia, because of its contribution to the mortality of malnourished children, its relatively wide extent, the dramatic irreversible damage (blindness) it causes and the possibilities for its prevention.

(c)   Nutritional anaemias because of their wide distribution, their contribution to the mortality from many other conditions and their repercussions on working capacity.

(d)   Endemic goitre because of its wide distribution and the effectiveness of low cost of prevention.

"I like John B. Seba
He is deep
     honest
     loving
     loyal
     funky
     free
     dedicated
     gentle
     American
     European
     cheerful
     thrifty
     brave
     clean and
     reverent
Also, far on.

What do we believe? Where are we? Where do we go?

HEADS

Hammerhead
Bulkhead
Warhead
Bighead
Leadhead
Redhead
Deadhead
Coolhead
Skinhead
Acidhead
Blockhead
Knothead
Warthead
Dumbhead
Pinhead
Fathead
Diamondhead
Knucklehead
Pothead
Goodhead
Juicehead
Lunkhead
Hardhead
Egghead
Squarehead
Flathead
Meathead
Bonehead
Stonehead
Maidenhead
Fountainhead
Featherhead
Worrywart
Copperhead
Steelhead
Woodhead
Sorehead
Drumhead
Wronghead
Godhead
Hothead
Barrelhead
Garbagehead
Woolhead
Jughead
Cylinderhead
Hogshead

Body Language That Says "Yes"

1. The buyer's breathing is smooth and steady
2. His voice is even-pitched, deep and warm
3. His eyes engage you for several seconds at a time and are fully visible
4. The head is held at the same level as yours
5. His forehead is smooth and un-furrowed
6. Hands and arms are relaxed and open
7. His gestures are smooth
8. His body is leaning forward slightly

Body Language That Says "No"

1. Breathing is short and quick
2. His voice is high-pitched and hesitant
3. The eyes avoid you. They either dart around or stare off into space
4. The head is down or held away from you
5. The forehead is creased and shows discomfort
6. Hands and arms are close to the body and may even be folded across the chest
7. The mouth is tight, smiles are forced
8. His gestures will be fast and un-even or nonexistent
9. His body will be held away from you and be rather rigid.

(Continued on page 20)

THE PROBLEM:

the only material that
for covers as
of State
was to
would be acceptable
compete with

Pastors

Rev. W. H.
Rev. Jason
Rev. Ebenezer
Rev. A. P.
Rev. David
Rev. B. F.
Rev. Ebenezer
Rev. W. H.
Rev. E. G.
Rev. G. S.
Rev. M. H.
Rev. R. L.
Rev. John
Rev. James
Rev. W. L.
Rev. J. W.
Rev. B. S.
Rev. Ernest
Rev. W. W.
Rev. W. P.
Rev. Howard
Rev. Oscar
Rev. L.
Rev. Leslie
Rev. John
Rev. Charles
Rev. C.
Rev. John
Rev. James
Rev. Chester
Rev. Cleaves

LEADER. Ladies and gentlemen, you are all invited to make a journey to any part of the world you may prefer, and tell me your mission; but you must name your destinations and errands in the order of the alphabet.

Miss A., where are you going?

ANS. To Alexandria.

LEADER. What will you do there?

ANS. Apply for Amusing Anecdotes.

"I am going to Baltimore," says the next.

LEADER. What will you do there?

ANS. Bake Bacon and Beans.

Each one is asked in turn by the leader, "Where are you going?" and "What will you do there?"

C—goes to Constantinople to Call for Citron.

D—to Danforth to Dress, Dine and Dance.

E—to Europe to Eagerly Enjoy Everything.

F—to Flanders to Fish for Flounders.

G—to Greenpoint to Garden and Groan.

H—to Hazlehurst to Hunt Hopping Hares.

I—to Ireland to Imitate Irishmen.

J—to Jersey to Join in a Jubilee.

K—to Kensington to Keep Kittens Kindly.

L—to Louisville to Love Loyally.

M—to Maryland to Marry a Musician.

N—to Newton to Nod Nervously.

O—to Ottawa to Own Outrageous Onions.

P—to Paterson to Patronize Pastry.

Q—to Queenstown to Quarrel Queerly.

R—to Rahway to Rove and Roam.

S—to Siam to Sell Seven Shawls.

T—to Toronto to Tell Tedious Tales.

U—to Uruguay to Upset a Usurper.

V—to Vienna to Vex a Vixen.

W—to Waterloo to Weep and Wail.

TIME'S NOW
INCREDIBLY SO

Now
you can have
the fastest most

Don't miss the excitement!
Don't miss the savings!
Don't miss anything!

we're
square

we
care

im·pos′si·ble (ĭm·pŏs′ĭ·b'l), *adj.*

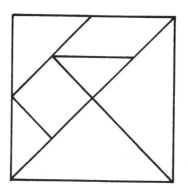

TONGUE TWISTER:

The crystal cherub's crown
charmed Charlotte.

HIJKKL
MMM
NOP

Tea

Althea Root Tea
Anise Seed Tea
Blueberry Leaf Tea
Buck Thorn Tea
Burdock Root Tea
Catnip Tea
Celery Seed Tea
Centaury Herb Tea
Cleavers Herb Tea
Corn Silk Tea
Couch Grass Tea
Dandelion Leaf Tea
Dogwood Bark Tea
Dulse Leaf Tea
Elder Flower Tea
Eucalyptus Tea
Eyebright Tea
Fennel Seed Tea
Gentian Root Tea
Golden Seal Herb Tea
Hops Tea
Horehound Herb Tea
Huckleberry Leaf Tea
Irish Moss Tea
Juniper Berry Tea
Kaffir Tea
Knot Grass Tea
Laurel Leaf Tea
Lavender Flower Tea
Licorice Root Tea
Linden Flower Tea
Mullein Leaf Tea
Parsley Tea
Pink Hybiscus Tea
Plantago Seed Tea
Plantain Tea
Princess Pine Tea
Rosemary Leaf Tea
Sage Tea
Scullcap Tea
Senna Leaf Tea
Slippery Elm Tea
St. John's Wort Tea
Strawberry Leaf Tea
Uva Ursi Tea
Violet Leaf Tea
Watercress Tea
White Oak Bark Tea
Yerba Santa Tea

American

☐ Please
☐ Please

☐ Please

☐ Please

☐ Alexander

☐ Clawson

☐ Cooper

☐ Hammond

☐ Schurr

☐ Govt.
☐ Please

Have
You
Listed
All Catalog Numbers?
All Colors?
All Sizes?

You're
Falling APART?

PORTER

YANKEE PIONEER

You should have found

1. ANAGRAMS
2. AUTHORS
3. BEAN BAG
4. BLINDMAN'S BUFF
5. BLOCKS
6. BLOWING BUBBLES
7. BUTTON, BUTTON
8. CATCH
9. CHECKERS
10. COLORING
11. COPS AND ROBBERS
12. COWBOYS AND INDIANS

13. CROQUET
14. DOMINOES
15. DRAWING
16. EGG HUNT
17. EMBROIDERY
18. ERECTOR
19. FLINCH
20. FOLLOW THE LEADER
21. GIANT STEP
22. HIDE AND SEEK
23. HOPSCOTCH
24. JACKS

25. JACKSTRAWS
26. JUMP ROPE
27. LEAPFROG
28. LONDON BRIDGE
29. LOTTO
30. MARBLES
31. MUSICAL CHAIRS
32. OLD MAID
33. ONE-O-CAT
34. PAINTING
35. POST OFFICE
36. RED LIGHT

37. RING AROUND THE ROSY
38. SIMON SAYS
39. SLEDDING
40. SKATE
41. STATUES
42. STEPS
43. TAG
44. TIC TAC TOE
45. TRADES
46. TUG-O-WAR
47. WINK

ATTACH LABEL HERE

7¢ TO 9¢
7½

7¢ TO 9¢
7½

33¢ TO 4

Is it important that a
married man be faithful?   Yes 96%
A married woman?   Yes 97

Yes 62
Yes 57

Yes 51

36

43

NOTE!
Follow the signs that read PLUM NEL

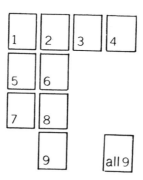

Enclosed.

STIMULATION: Kissing, pulling, pinching, rolling, licking, patting, squeezing, flicking, scratching, reaming, stroking, caressing, sucking, nipping, shaking, enpalming, swallowing, rubbing, blowing . . .

```
7.  7 married couples ....14
    3 widows ........... 3
    12 bachelors .........12
    10 girls ............10
                         ──
                         39 people.
```

25mpg is lousy

yes! PLEASE
RUSH...

young

525529

525766

525545

525588

525448

525731

525480

525855

525804

525650

525405

525901

country years	1969	1968	1967
Japan	28	20	14
U.S.A.	19	22	25
Italy	18	20	21
West Germany	13	13	13
Sweden	6	7	8
Argentina	4	4	4
Switzerland	3	3	3
Denmark	2	3	2
United Kingdom	2	2	2
Other Countries	5	6	8

ELASTIC STOCKINGS

51 Gauge Nylon—Full Fashion
Sheer Deluxe Nylon—Fashioned

R-2 Above Knee, Full Foot ....

U-2 Ultra Sheer ....

S-2 Above Knee, Full Foot ....

J-2 Seamless, Above Knee, Full Foot

Nylon—Fashioned

N-1 Above Knee, Open Toe ....

N-3 Below Knee, Open Toe ....

N-2 Above Knee, Full Foot ....

Cotton—Fashioned

L-1 Above Knee, Open Toe ....

L-3 Below Knee, Open Toe ....

Men's Nylon

A-4 Below Knee, Full Foot,
   Brown or Black ....

* I have seen it relieve crippled hands and feet, caused by painful arthritis, straighten whole bodies and bring them back to normal!

* It can stop the pain of hemorrhoids almost immediately!

* Most headaches vanish immediately with this method!

* I have seen it relieve liver and gall bladder trouble!

* I have seen it clear up stuffed sinuses almost immediately!

* I have seen it relieve back troubles, in a matter of seconds!

* I have seen it bring fast relief to stomach troubles!

* I have brought lasting relief to sufferers of varicose veins with this method. This is also true with cramps or pains in the legs!

* I have seen it relieve bladder trouble quickly, with great relief after the very first treatment -- all sensation of burning or itching seem to disappear completely!

IF YOU ARE HAVING
BIG
PROBLEMS
WITH SMALL
THEN YOU SHOULD DIAL
(617) 891-5230
AND DISCUSS YOUR
PROBLEM
WITH THE ENGINEERS
WHO DESIGN AND BUILD

A — rhomboid dodecaëder; B — deltoid dodecaëder; C — pentagon dodecaëder; D — pyramide cube; E — icosite-traëder; F — tetraëdric pentagon dodecaëder; G — disdo-decaëder; H — hexakistetroëder; I — pentagon icosite-traëder; J — hexakisoctaëder.

A   B   C   D   E

F   G   H   I   K

RULES FOR CLASSES 1-7

1. Keep your hands at your sides.
2. Raise your hand to speak.
3. Be polite and kind to all.
4. Fold hands when not working

Distance
up to 3 miles
up to 2 miles

RD REN   - - - EARLY BIRD REN   - - - EARLY
EWAL NO   - - - EARLY BIRD RENEWAL NO   - - - EARLY BIRD REN

Basic
School
School

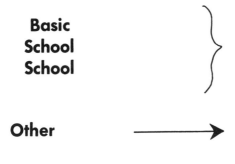

Other

Basic
School

All Other

Reflections

$$a > 2\frac{I}{\mu}$$

(A)

$$a < 2\frac{I}{\mu}$$

$$a > 2\frac{I}{\mu}$$

(B)

$$a < 2\frac{I}{\mu}$$

$$a > 2\frac{I}{\mu}$$

OFFER

Purchase the GBC

OFFER

Purchase a GBC

OFFER

Purchase a GBC :

OFFER

Purchase a GBC

HIGH VOLTAGE

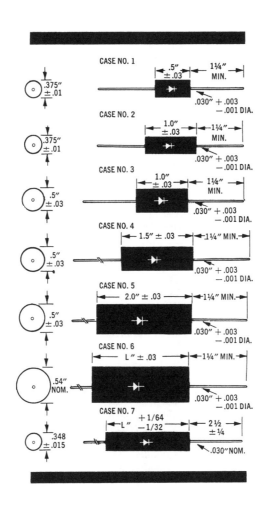

CASE NO. 1

.375″ ±.01

.5″ ±.03

1¼″ MIN.

.030″ + .003 − .001 DIA.

CASE NO. 2

.375″ ±.01

1.0″ ±.03

1¼″ MIN.

.030″ + .003 − .001 DIA.

CASE NO. 3

.5″ ±.03

1.0″ ±.03

1¼″ MIN.

.030″ + .003 − .001 DIA.

CASE NO. 4

.5″ ±.03

1.5″ ± .03

1¼″ MIN.

.030″ + .003 − .001 DIA.

CASE NO. 5

.5″ ±.03

2.0″ ± .03

1¼″ MIN.

.030″ + .003 − .001 DIA.

CASE NO. 6

.54″ NOM.

L″ ± .03

1¼″ MIN.

.030″ + .003 − .001 DIA.

CASE NO. 7

.348 ±.015

L″ + 1/64 − 1/32

2½ ±¼

.030″ NOM.

DESCRIPTION

WALL, SINGLE WIDE
WALL, DOUBLE WIDE
ISLAND, SINGLE WIDE
ISLAND, SINGLE WIDE
ISLAND, SINGLE WIDE
ISLAND, SINGLE WIDE
ISLAND, DOUBLE WIDE
ISLAND, DOUBLE WIDE
ISLAND, DOUBLE WIDE
ISLAND, DOUBLE WIDE

WALL, SINGLE WIDE
WALL, DOUBLE WIDE
ISLAND, SINGLE WIDE
ISLAND, SINGLE WIDE
ISLAND, SINGLE WIDE
ISLAND, SINGLE WIDE
ISLAND, DOUBLE WIDE
ISLAND, DOUBLE WIDE
ISLAND, DOUBLE WIDE
ISLAND, DOUBLE WIDE

WALL, SINGLE WIDE
WALL, DOUBLE WIDE
ISLAND, SINGLE WIDE
ISLAND, SINGLE WIDE
ISLAND, SINGLE WIDE
ISLAND, SINGLE WIDE
ISLAND, DOUBLE WIDE
ISLAND, DOUBLE WIDE
ISLAND, DOUBLE WIDE
ISLAND, DOUBLE WIDE

the series

Number One :
Number Two :
Number Three :
Number Four :
Number Five :

Number Six :

Number Seven :
Number Eight :

Number Nine :
Number Ten :

Number Eleven :
Number Twelve :

two:

One is

The other is

Whichever

versatility

- sorted
- first in, first out
- last in, first out
- random

the priorities

```
5. Sex
4. Food
3. H₂O
2. O₂
1. God
```

the office nearest you:

. . . . (312) 271-1464

. . . . (213) 472-3452

. . . . (314) 727-2345

. . . . (212) 661-0370

. . . . (413) 536-7800

Another
Billy
Blaze
Blaze
Blaze
Blaze
Blaze
Blaze
Blaze
Blaze
Blaze
Blaze

All you have to do is: 1 Circle the

2 Fill in

3 Tear out and

EXAMPLES:
(Flexible portion

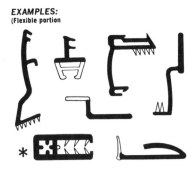

Left Hand and Right Hand

20″	14 Thru 23	4	Bronze	LH-RH
19″	14 Thru 23	4	Bronze	LH-RH
18″	14 Thru 21	4	Bronze	LH-RH

Money Horse

Oct. 3	No. 1	SIXTH
Oct. 4	No. 2	SIXTH
Oct. 5	No. 8	FIRST
Oct. 6	No. 7	THIRD
Oct. 7	No. 6	FIFTH
Oct. 8	No. 5	SEVENTH
Oct. 9	No. 4	NINTH

Fixed Bed	Moving Bed
FAIR TO POOR	**HIGH**
HIGH	**LOW**
LOW	**HIGH**
NO	**YES**
High Cubic Footage	**Low Cubic Footage High Headroom**
YES	**NO**

Deck
---

two, three, four
two
two, three,
   four, five
one, two,
   three, four
two
three, four
two, three,
   four, five
two
one, three, four
two, three, five
two, four
three, four,
   five
one, two, three,
   four, five
two, four
two, three,
   five
two, five

four

five

The 89 offenses I committed, the 502 times I committed them, plus the implication that I enjoyed myself thoroughly with every act on every occasion and would repeat any or all of them whenever the chance arises.

1.	Aggravated Assault	1
2.	Attempt to Illuminate Wild Game	5
3.	Attempted Larceny	1
4.	Attempted Larceny of a M/V	4
5.	Assault on a Police Officer	1
6.	Assault with Intent to Kill	1
7.	Assault and Battery	9
8.	A.W.O.L	11
9.	Break & Entering	7
10.	Break & Entering in the Night Time	1
11.	Break & Entering & Larceny in the Night Time	4
12.	Bench Warrants	2
13.	Break & Entering with Intent	9
14.	Break & Entering & Larceny	13
15.	Behaving in an Incorrigible Manner	1
16.	Break & Entering in the Day Time	1
17.	Concealing Stolen Property	2
18.	Conspiracy	2
19.	Capias Executions	3
20.	Cheating by False Pretenses	6
21.	Carrying a Concealed Weapon	2
22.	Driving while Impaired	30
23.	Driving to Endanger	4
24.	Drinking in a Public Place	11
25.	Disorderly Conduct	33
26.	Defrauding an Inn Keeper	1
27.	Disturbing the Peace	2
28.	Driving an Unregistered Motor Vehicle	1
29.	Escape	2
30.	Failure to Stop for an Officer	3
31.	Failure to Report an Accident	1
32.	Felonious Assault	1
33.	Fishing Without a License	1
34.	Fugitive from Justice	2
35.	Failure to Keep to the Right	1
36.	Grand Larceny	2
37.	Habeas Corpus	4
38.	Hitch Hiking	3
39.	Hunting in a Closed Season	1
40.	Intoxication	56
41.	Intoxicated in a Home	1
42.	Indecent Liberties	2
43.	Idle & Disorderly	1
44.	Intent to Defraud	1
45.	Interferring with a Police Officer	1
46.	Illegal Tran. of Intoxicating Liquor	19

40.	Intoxication	56
41.	Intoxicated in a Home	1
42.	Indecent Liberties	2
43.	Idle & Disorderly	1
44.	Intent to Defraud	1
45.	Interferring with a Police Officer	1
46.	Illegal Tran. of Intoxicating Liquor	19
47.	Illegal Possession of Intoxicating Liquor	25
48.	Intoxicated on the Highway	1
49.	Intoxicated on a Street	2
50.	Intoxicated in a Motor Vehicle	19
51.	Intoxicated in a Public Place	17
52.	Kidnapping	1
53.	Loitering	1
54.	Larceny	2
55.	Leaving the Scene of an Accident	2
56.	Littering	3
57.	Lodgers	3
58.	Making an unnecessary Noise with a M/V	2
59.	Malicious Mischief	4
60.	Mental Illness	1
61.	Non-Support	1
62.	Operating while Impaired	7
63.	Operating a M/V to Endanger	1
64.	Operating a Motor Bike W/O Head Gear	1
65.	Operating a M/V Without a License	15
66.	Operating a Motor Cycle While Impaired	1
67.	Operating a M/V After Suspension	13
68.	Possession of Deer in a Closed Season	4
69.	Procurring Liquor for a Minor	2
70.	Passing on a Hill	1
71.	Possession of Stolen Property	2
72.	Reckless Driving	4
73.	Receiving Stolen Goods	3
74.	Rape	4
75.	Resisting Arrest	3
76.	Surrender of Bail	1
77.	Speeding	6
78.	Stop Sign Violation	2
79.	Simple Larceny	1
80.	Trespass in a Building	1
81.	Threatening Communication	1
82.	Threatening a Police Officer	2
83.	Tampering with a Motor Vehicle	1
84.	Taking a Motor Vehicle W/O Owners Consent	13
85.	Uttering a Forged Instrument	14
86.	Violation of Probation	17
87.	Violation of Parole	2
88.	Vandalism	1
89.	Vexation	1
	Total	502

a primer for the uninitiated:

	G.B.	U.S.
Aid.	First.	Foreign.
Black.	Black.	This year's tactful word for Negro.
Dame.	Barbara Wootton.	A dame.
Dry Martini.	Not much Martini vermouth.	No Martini vermouth.
Greeks.	Diogenes, Demosthenes.	Delicatessens.
Mafia.	Sicilian thuggery, drugs, gambling.	Big business.
Stay, You Must Come And Stay With Us.	For the past twenty years you have behaved surprisingly well for an American, so I don't suppose you'll break anything or embarrass us if you spend the weekend with us.	Having known you for over five minutes, I'd be delighted to ask you for the weekend as long as you move on afterwards.
Riot.	Two in the hospital, three windows broken, British way of life in danger.	Four dead, a hundred injured, life as usual.
Well.	Well, you know, the thing is . . .	Oil.

7 major problems

1. The Boredom Problem

2. The Time Problem

3. The Cost Problem

4. The Speed Problem

5. The Retention Problem

6. The Space Problem

7. The Manpower Problem

the   priorities

5. Sex
4. Food
3. H_2O
2. O_2
1. God

the office nearest you:

. . . . (312) 271-1464

. . . . (213) 472-3452

. . . . (314) 727-2345

. . . . (212) 661-0370

. . . . (413) 536-7800

 *Ride*

 *Stack*

 *Walk*

 *All three*

DO EVERYTHING

Hours

Noon to 6 pm
Noon to 6 pm
Noon to 6 pm
Noon to 6 pm

SAFE, SURE, SPEEDY ITCH

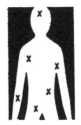

EXAMPLE:

1. shook with fear
2. sat restlessly
3. turned swiftly around
4. spoke loudly
5. fell hard

OPEN SATURDAY

9

UNTIL

12

NORTHWEST OFFICE

3. A circle.
4. A line.
5. A tiger's nail or claw.
6. A peacock's foot.
7. The jump of a hare.
8. The leaf of a blue lotus.
1. Sounding.
2. Half moon.

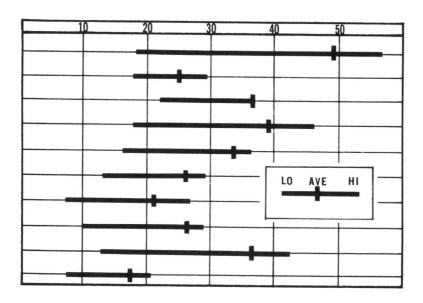

THIS IS
YOUR
LUCKY
COMBINATION

Do You Want to Know What These Represent?

BALLOTS	RETAIN
PENNTAP	JITCO
EPIC	BARC
MEDLARS	MERC
ERIC	PRISE
MARC	SCANDOC
GEO-REF	JILA
NELINET	LADS
DATRIX	COSMIC
ORBIT	FoIC
LEADERMART	LEADS
LARC	ASIS
CARDS	ANALYTS
NOAA	COMPENDEX
BIOSIS	SCAN
ISI	COSATI
POST-J	LOLITA
BIBLIOFILE	RICE

GLUMP

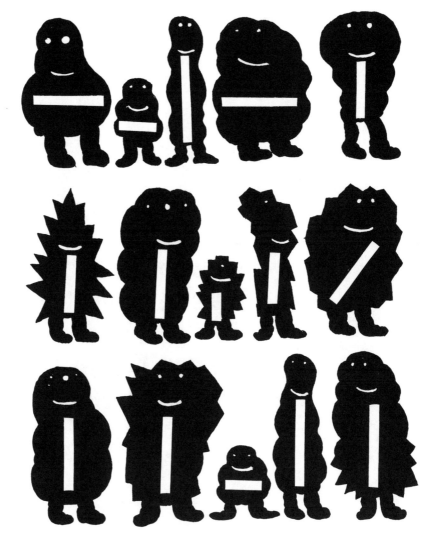

All these creatures are Glumps.

None of these creatures is a Glump.

Which of these are Glumps?

are electrically identical*
are mechanically identical*
are functionally identical*

shave

We don't drag
We don't roar
We don't roll
We don't flip
We don't float
We don't raise
We don't lower

Symbol
V_{DI}
I_{DI}
R_{in}
I_{in}
V_{CMI}
C_{MRR}
A_{VOL}
V_{OM}
P_D
e_n
ΔV_{DI}
V_{SRR}
TC_{Iio}

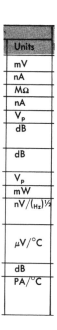

Units
mV
nA
$M\Omega$
nA
V_P
dB
dB
V_P
mW
$nV/(_{Hz})^{1/2}$
$\mu V/^\circ C$
dB
$PA/^\circ C$

E means Early;
L means Late.

*Barley
*Beans (E)
    (L)
Beets (E)
    (L)
*Broccoli (E)
    (L)
*Brussels Spr.
*Cabbage Pl. (E)
    (L)
Carrots (E)
    (L)
*Cauliflower Pl. (E)
    (L)
Celery (E)
    (L)
*Corn, Sw. (E)
    (L)
*Cucumber
*Eggplant Pl.
Endive (E)
    (L)
*Flowers (All)
*Kale (E)
    (L)
Leek Pl.
*Lettuce
*Melon (Musk)
Onion Pl.
*Parsley
Parsnip
*Peas (E)
    (L)
*Pepper Pl.
Potato
*Pumpkin
Radish (E)
    (L)
*Spinach (E)
    (L)
*Summer Squash
*Swiss Chard
*Tomato Pl.
Turnip (E)
    (L)
*Wheat (Winter)
    (Spring)

Snow Leopard

- 1 snow leopard, dried and frozen
- 6 gallons Nanga Parbat consommé
- 14 pine cones, peeled and seeded
- 2 pounds locust wings
- 2 tablespoons *hangul*
- 2 tablespoons *serow*
- 2 tablespoons *goral*
- 2 tablespoons *tahr*
- 2 tablespoons kosher salt
- pinch of monosodium glutamate
- grass, any common or garden variety, to taste

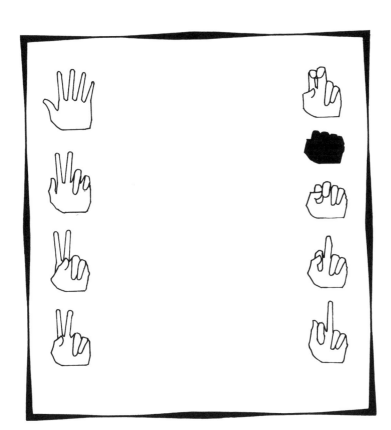

Porter Takes Over At Pea

priority:

☐......Hung-up? ....☐
☐......Fed-up? ....☐
☐......Down-trodden? ....☐
☐......Up-tight? ....☐
☐......Underpaid? ....☐
☐......Overworked? ....☐
☐......On the Pill? ....☐
☐......Enrolled in Karate school? ....☐
☐......Out to lunch? ....☐
☐......Married and happy ever after? ....☐
☐......Married and miserable?..................☐
☐......Unmarried and unhappy? ....☐
☐......Candidate for Witch? ....☐
☐......Member of Women's Liberation Front?.....☐
☐......Too busy to say?......................☐

security

1) Security from hunger
2) Security from violence
3) Security of health
4) Security from climatic extremes
5) Security of the night for procreation
6) Security of the offspring
7) Security of old age.

RANGE OF USEFULNESS
5-UP
5-UP
5-UP
5-UP
5-UP
5-UP
5-UP
5-UP
5-UP
5-UP
5-UP
5-UP
5-UP
5-UP

In one poll, he ranked two places behind Jesus Christ

Al
see
he
do
int
Ac
$3,
ph
do
a t
ria
wit
die
bis

All-in-one

Wisdom comes in b i t s and p i e c e s

Just as it is learned.

No one gets b i g chunks o f it.

That's not how it's earned.

Aspect

II. THE QUEST
    a. distinctive
       power motives

    b. destruction of
       friends

III. MAN, AS THE
    a. material success,
       spiritual failure

    b. combines power
       with spiritual
       and love
       problems

    c. misers of
       material things

    d. material failures,
       spiritual success

    e. artist in society

IV. ABERRANTS
    a. pathological

    b. archetypal
       figures

The sound Hin.
The thundering sound.
The cooing sound.
The weeping sound.
The sound Phut.
The sound Phat.
The sound Sut.
The sound Plat.

7:15 P. M.

Miss Carol Elwell
"He Lives" - by Ackley

"My Sins Are Gone" - by Vandall
Mrs. John MacNeill
Rev. John MacNeill
Rev. John MacNeill
No. 406
Mrs. John MacNeill
Rev. Chester Staples
No. 100

High Pass
$\dfrac{\omega_o}{p}$
$-\dfrac{\omega_o}{\omega}$
$\dfrac{\dfrac{p}{\omega_o{}'}}{1 + \dfrac{p}{\omega_o{}'}}$
$\dfrac{\left(\dfrac{p}{\omega_o{}'}\right)^2}{1 + 2\xi_L\dfrac{p}{\omega_o{}'} + \left(\dfrac{p}{\omega_o{}'}\right)^2}$
$\omega_o{}' = \dfrac{\omega_c}{\omega_L}\omega_o$

multiples

0404 Capricorn
0405 Aquarius
0406 Pisces
0407 Aries
0408 Taurus
0409 Gemini

0410 Cancer
0411 Leo
0412 Virgo
0413 Libra
0414 Scorpio
0415 Sagittarius

A CHILD

nano

A shortcut through

the basement.

Isolated buried layer

transisto

invented

ama

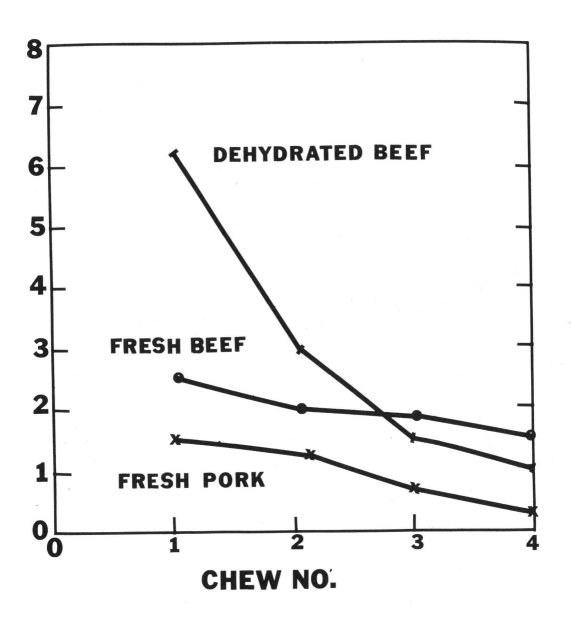

NOISE
& SHOUTING
& hoopla

3-5250

3-5252

3-5254

3-5255

3-5260

3-5262

3-5268

3-5271

3-5272

3-5273

3-5274

3-5275

3-5276

3-5282

3-5283

3-5284

3-5285

3-5287
257

3-5288

3-5289

The
quietest

you
can get

Look!

PLACE YOUR FINGER HERE

ACTUAL SIZE

AND PUSH!

YOU HAVE JUST PUSHED

Easy, wasn't it?

PUSH-BUTTON

Now stop pushing...

WAYS

They're all one

S A B R E with C
S A B R E with I
S A B R E with I
S A B R E with D
S A B R E with D
S A B R E with V
S A B R E with K
S A B R E with K
S A B R E with L
S A B R E with T
S A B R E with Z

Success

Family car
Firm car
Theatre car
Party car
Vacation car
Business car
Airport car
Dockside car
Day car
Weekend car
Weekly car
Monthly car

NOTHING TO ADD
NOTHING TO ADD
NOTHING TO ADD
NOTHING TO ADD
NOTHING TO ADD
NOTHING TO ADD
NOTHING TO ADD
NOTHING TO ADD
NOTHING TO ADD

1. Racial Situation
2. High Taxes
3. Crowded Schools
4. Water Shortage
5. Slum Clearance

1. Racial Situation
2. Crowded Schools
3. Unemployment
4. Need for Higher Salaries
5. Juvenile Delinquency

1. Racial Situation
2. High Taxes
3. Crowded Schools
4. Police Protection
5. Need for More Industry

1. Racial Situation
2. Unemployment
3. High Taxes
4. Traffic Congestion
5. Water Shortage

Rating.
No Rating
No Rating
★★★
★★
★★★
★
No Rating
No Rating
No Rating

Who knows <u>more</u> about

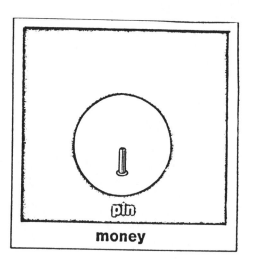

pin

money

9

Are You Going To Move?

(03) ⬜⬜⬜⬜⬜⬜⬜⬜⬜⬜⬜⬜⬜⬜⬜⬜⬜⬜⬜⬜⬜⬜⬜⬜⬜⬜⬜⬜⬜⬜⬜⬜
(First Name, Middle Initial, Last Name)

(04) ⬜⬜⬜⬜⬜⬜⬜⬜⬜⬜⬜⬜⬜⬜⬜⬜⬜⬜⬜⬜⬜⬜⬜⬜⬜⬜⬜⬜⬜⬜⬜⬜
(Extra Address Line — Use only if necessary)

(05) ⬜⬜⬜⬜⬜⬜⬜⬜⬜⬜⬜⬜⬜⬜⬜⬜⬜⬜⬜⬜⬜⬜⬜⬜⬜⬜⬜⬜⬜⬜⬜⬜
(No. and Street)

(06) ⬜⬜⬜⬜⬜⬜⬜⬜⬜⬜⬜⬜⬜⬜⬜⬜⬜⬜⬜⬜⬜⬜⬜⬜⬜⬜⬜ (07) ⬜⬜⬜⬜⬜
(City and State)   (ZIP)

— Office Use Only —

(01) ⬜⬜⬜⬜⬜ (02) C

(09) ⬜⬜⬜

it's easy to put your finger

**Spray, spread, cast,
caulk or pour these**

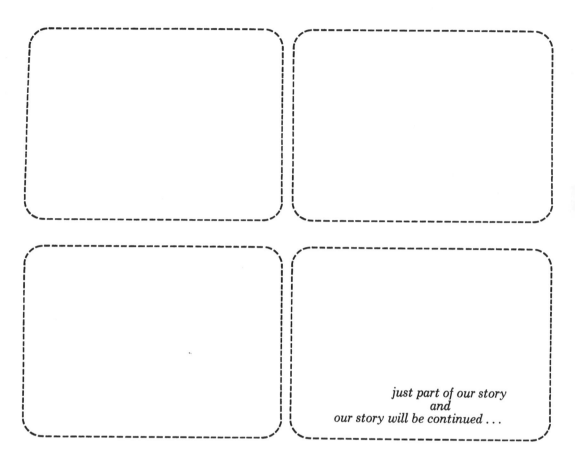

just part of our story
and
our story will be continued . . .

THIS IS   **THIS IS TOO!**

**CO-
OPERATIVE**
40.0%
18.6
11.8
8.3
5.
8.3
5.
—
.8
.8
1.6
—
—
—
—
—

NUMBER SIGNS

# # # # # # #

CHECK MARKS

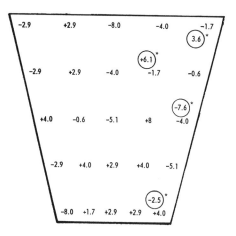

THE FOURTH EVENING.

LEADER. I planted my *Shakspeare*, and it came up *Sweet William*.

FIRST PLAYER. I planted *men and women*, and they came up *beans* (beings).

SECOND. I planted *Rover*, and he came up *dog-wood*.

THIRD. I planted a *coquette*, and she came up *love-in-a-maze*.

FOURTH. I planted a *battle*, and there came up *flags*.

FIFTH. I planted a *widow*, and she came up *weeds*.

SIXTH. I planted a *fop*, and he came up *dandelion*.

SEVENTH. I planted *Coney Island*, and it came up *beech*.

EIGHTH. I planted a *negro*, and he came up *tulips* (two lips).

NINTH. I planted an *English coin*, and it came up *penny royal*.

TENTH. I planted a *young fowl*, and it came up *chick-weed*.

ELEVENTH. I planted a *fast young man*, and he came up *wild oats*.

TWELFTH. I planted a *cigar*, and it came up *ashes*.

THIRTEENTH. I planted *vain wishes*, and they came up *sour grapes*.

FOURTEENTH. I planted *charity*, and it came up *hearts-ease*.

FIFTEENTH. I planted a *kid*, and it came up *lady-slipper*.

SIXTEENTH. I planted a *clock*, and it came up *thyme*.

SEVENTEENTH. I planted a *philosopher*, and he came up *sage*.

EIGHTEENTH. I planted a *defeated candidate*, and he came up *beet*.

Figure
action

● nitroglycerin retard tablet swallowed intact
▲ nitroglycerin retard tablet cut into 2 parts
■ nitroglycerin retard tablet cut into 4 parts
○ nitroglycerin retard tablet powdered

RUBBER BANDS

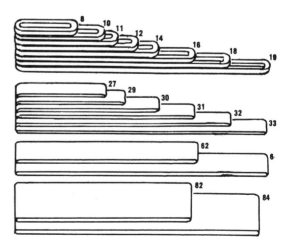

January—It is hard to get a living.

February—Moon in which there is crust on the snow.

March—Moon in which the hens lay.

April—Moon in which we catch fish.

May—Moon in which we sow.

June—Moon in which we catch young seals.

July—Moon in which the berries are ripe.

August—Moon in which there is a heap of eels on the sand.

September — Moon in which there are herds of moose, bears, etc.

October—There is ice on the banks.

November—Moon in which the frost fish comes.

December—The long moon.

RESULT:

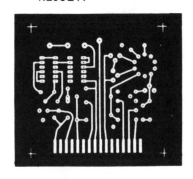 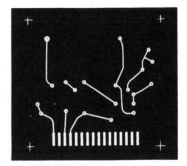

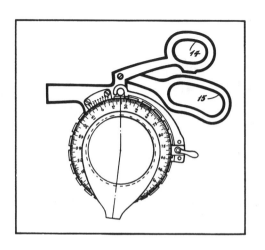

Here, for your enjoyment, are a few square inches of quiet. Rest
your eyes here . . . rest your ears in a   Take a Quiet
Break at
"We'll be here tomorrow

A	G	N	A
H	A	R	T
T	E	M	S

SALE

          stuff, skirts, pants, casual dress-
es, tee shirts, etc., etc., etc., etc., etc.,
etc., etc., etc., etc., etc., etc., etc.,
etc., etc., etc., etc., etc., etc., etc.,
etc., etc., etc., etc., etc., etc., etc.,
etc., etc., etc., etc., etc., etc., etc.,
etc., etc., etc., etc., etc., etc., etc.,
etc., etc., etc., etc., etc., etc., etc.,
etc., etc., etc., etc., etc., etc., etc.,

COMING SOON
h

STOCK

STAINLESS STEEL
BRASS
BRONZE
ALUMINUM
MONEL
NYLON

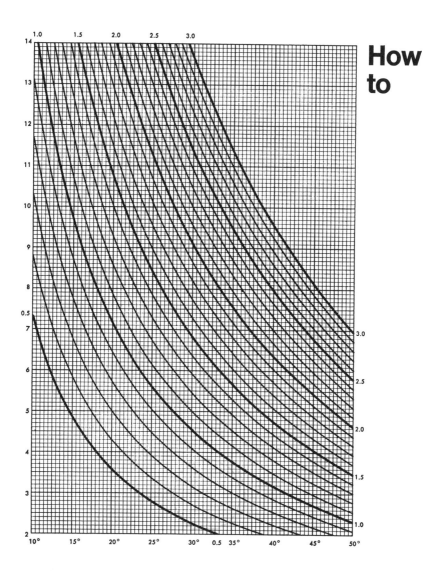

dual integrated mos chopper

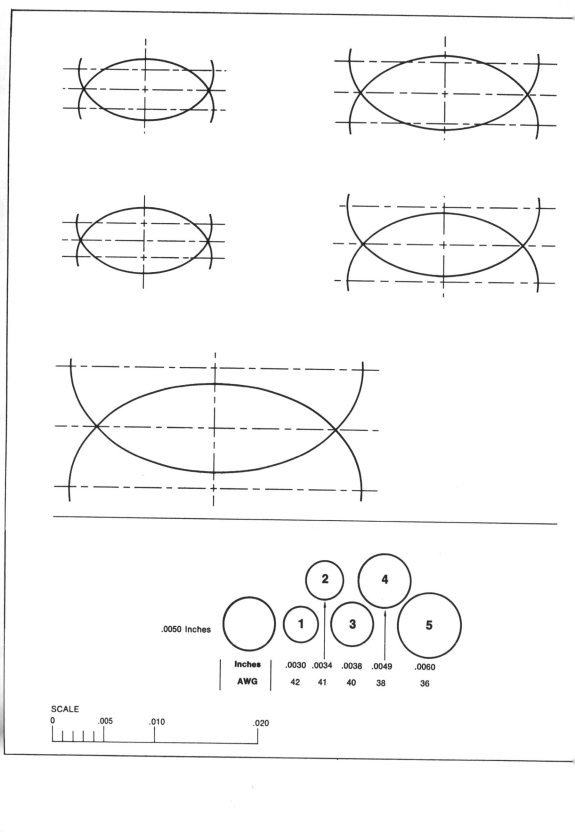

.0050 Inches

Inches	.0030	.0034	.0038	.0049	.0060
AWG	42	41	40	38	36

SCALE

0   .005   .010   .020

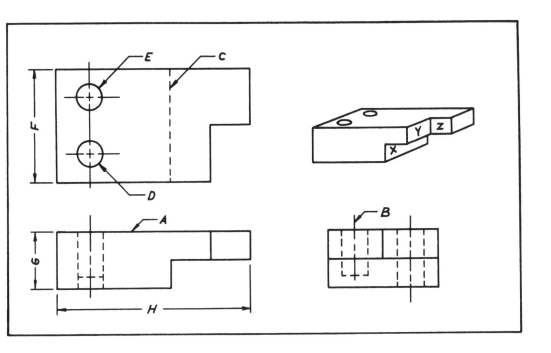

1. What kind of line is indicated by A? _____

2. What kind of line is indicated by B? _____

3. What kind of line is indicated by C? _____

4. Which view shows surface X? _____

5. Which view shows surface Y? _____

6. Which view shows surface Z? _____

7. Which hole is drilled "through" (E or D)? _____

8. What letter represents the length? _____

9. What letter represents the width? _____

10. What letter represents the thickness? _____

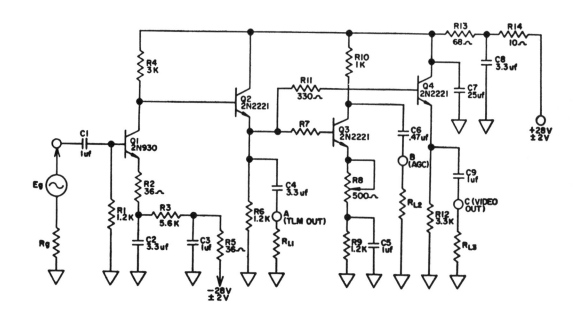

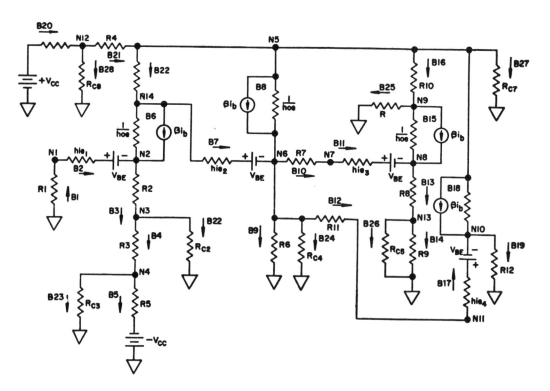

NOW IT CAN BE

heya

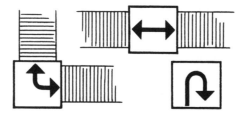

Plug/Cable
Plug/Cable
Plug/Cable
Jack/Cable
Jack/Cable
Right Angle, Plug/Cable
Right Angle, Plug/Cable
Right Angle, Plug/Cable

Plug/Cable
Right Angle, Plug/Cable
Right Angle, Plug/Cable
Right Angle, Plug/Cable
Plug/Cable
Plug/Cable
Plug/Cable
Flange Mount, Jack/Cable
Flange Mount, Jack/Cable
Flange Mount, Jack/Cable

Bulkhead Feedthrough,
Jack/Jack, Pressurized
Bulkhead Feedthrough,
Jack/Jack
Adapter, Straight, Jack/Jack
Adapter, Straight, Plug/Plug
Adapter, Right Angle,
Plug/Jack

Small Boat to Luxembourg

Small Boat

Small Boat

SMALL BOAT IN SOUTHERN FRANCE
SMALL BOAT ON THE THAMES
SMALL BOAT THROUGH BELGIUM
SMALL BOAT THROUGH FRANCE
SMALL BOAT THROUGH GERMANY
SMALL BOAT THROUGH HOLLAND
SMALL BOAT ON THE MEUSE
SMALL BOAT TO ALSACE
SMALL BOAT TO BAVARIA
SMALL BOAT THROUGH THE SKAGERRAK

```
          A
        B in A
I       C in B       Long
        D in C       Short
         Total


          A
        B in A
II      C in B       Long
        D in C       Short
         Total



          A
        B in A
III     C in B       Long
        D in C       Short
         Total


          A
        B in A
IV      C in B       Long
        D in C       Short
         Total
```

CO_2 LN_2 LH_2

3 new

SELECTION

Yes	Yes	Yes	Yes	Limited	Yes	No	Yes	No	Yes	Yes	✓
Yes	Yes	Yes	Yes	Limited	Yes	Yes	Yes	Yes	Yes	Yes	✓
Yes	Yes	Limited	Yes	Limited	Yes	Yes	Yes	Yes	Yes	Yes	✓
Yes	Yes	Limited	Yes	Limited	Yes	Yes	Yes	Yes	Yes	Yes	✓
No	Yes	Limited	Yes	Yes	Yes	Yes	Yes	No	No	No	No
Yes	Yes	Limited	Yes	Limited	Yes	Yes	Yes	Yes	No	Yes	✓
Yes	Yes	Yes	Yes	Limited	Yes	No	Yes	No	No	Yes	✓
Yes	Yes	Limited	Yes	No	Yes	Yes	Yes	Yes	No	Yes	✓
Yes	Yes	Limited	Yes	No	Yes	No	Yes	No	Limited	Yes	✓
Yes	Yes	Limited	Yes	No	Yes	No	Yes	No	Limited	Yes	✓
Yes	Yes	Limited	Yes	No	Yes	No	Yes	No	Limited	Yes	✓
Yes	Yes	Yes	Yes	No	Yes	No	Yes	No	Yes	Yes	✓
Yes	Yes	Limited	Yes	No	Yes	No	Yes	No	Yes	Yes	✓
Yes	Yes	Limited	Yes	No	Yes	No	Yes	No	Yes	Yes	✓
Yes	Yes	Yes	Yes	Yes	Yes	No	Yes	No	Yes	Yes	✓
Yes	Yes	Yes	Yes	Yes	Yes	Yes	Yes	Yes	Yes	Yes	✓
Yes	Yes	Limited	Yes	No	Yes	Yes	Yes	Yes	Limited	Yes	✓
Yes	No	No	No	No	No	No	No	No	No	Yes	No
Yes	No	No	No	No	No	No	No	No	No	Yes	No
No	Yes	Limited	Yes	Yes	Yes	Yes	Yes	Yes	No	No	No
Yes	Yes	Yes	Yes	Yes	Yes	Yes	Yes	Yes	Yes	Yes	✓
Yes	Yes	Yes	Yes	No	Yes	Yes	Yes	Yes	Limited	Yes	✓

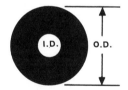

I.D. O.D.

We fire people.

And they love it. Because

Who? What? Where? When? Why?

Read Every day.

Yes.
No.
All right.
Please. (take this or have this)
Sorry!
Good morning!
Hello!
Good evening.
Good night.
How are you?
Good-bye!
See you again!

Thank you.
Wait a moment!
I beg your pardon!
You're welcome.
What's the matter?
Do you understand?
Yes, I understand.
No, I don't understand.
What time is it now?
What a shame!
Really?
Hey great! , Wow!

HIGH

DTL INT

☐

☐ High

☐ High

☐ Low
function.

☐ Fan-out: 8

☐ Single and double

☐ Dual source
for pin basis

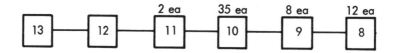

PHASE IV

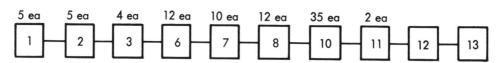

EXPLODES   tides
and   torrents   and   pinwheels-
bobsblotchessprays-   spurtsre-
dorangeyel-
lowblueshapesbeyond
                WORDS
   rotatingthrob-
bingthrash-
ingspinning-
dancingGROWINGshrinking   al-
latonce   and   the   kidsintheau-
dience
                LOSE
   their egos in the sublime ex-
cess and sit narcotized with
hardly a head nod or a foot
stomp and
                HOLD
   the arms of their seats and
suddenly it is all over.

PHASES I, II, III

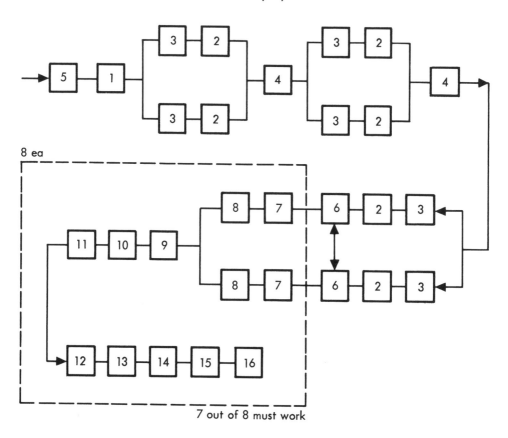

8 ea

7 out of 8 must work

PHASE IV

SCIENCES

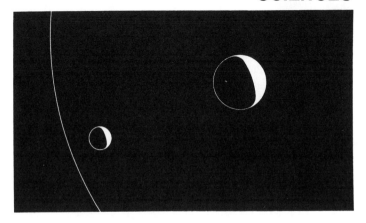

EARTH, MOON, AND PLANETS

THE THING

POSTERIOR

LATERAL

SITTING

STANDING

WHERE: On bed, chair, desk, table, floor, wall, beach, ocean, field, forest, car . . .

L
NS

PUSH BUTTON SWITCHES.
WIPING,SNAP ACTION
AND BUTT CONTACTS.
SPST.SPDT.DPST.DPDT.
PUSH-PULL.LIGHTED.
25,000 to 1,000,000

WHAT'S TCA?

ASK UA-TW-PA-EA-DL-AA

Advertise   **for Quick New**

USE THIS HANDY

(PLEASE PRINT NEATLY)

(We reserve right to edit copy)

Age	State	Occupation	Color Hair $	Color-Eyes	Height
Weight	Religion	Birthdate	Income	per	Make car
Value	Home	Years of	School/College	Widowed or	Divorced/single
other	information	other	information	other	information
would you	prefer to	become	acquainted	with.	etc.

High Life

The **MASO**

you can
cut it...
drill it...
rout it...
mill it...
tap it...
shape it...

$$610$$

$$633$$

$$663$$

it all adds up

read

1. this year said steve im really enjoying english and social studies
2. my mother heard superintendent burke say that he and mrs burke will take a trip through the south during the summer
3. yes i bought twenty three marbles for $120 (one dollar and twenty cents).
4. at 130 P M dr h b williams will talk to our class about his new book on the road to better health
5. you will of course be expected to bring your own plates glasses and silverware

It looks ★ but it's ★★★.

Do You Think Straight?

Answers
test on

One)   1—T;   Two)   1—F;
Three) 1—F, 2—T; Four) 1—F;
Five) 1—F, 2—T; Six) 1—F,
2—F, 3—T; Seven) 1—F;
Eight) 1—T, 2—F; Nine) 1—F,
2—F, 3—T; Ten) 1—F, 2—T,
3—F; Eleven) 1—F, 2—F, 3—
T.

Twelve) 1—F, 2—F, 3—T;
Thirteen) 1—F, 2—F, 3—T;
Fourteen) 1—F, 2—F, 3—T;
Fifteen) 1—T, 2—F, 3—F; Six-
teen) 1—T, 2—F, 3—F; Seven-
teen) 1—F, 2—F, 3—T; Eigh-
teen) 1—T, 2—F; Nineteen)
1—F, 2—F, 3—F; Twenty)
1—F, 2—F, 3—T.

BRACES

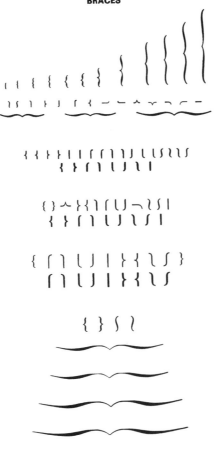

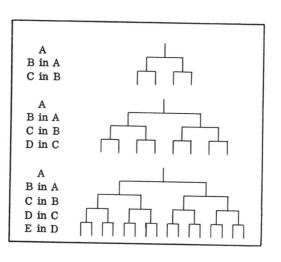

word game

Wraps:
Broadside:
Broadside:
Wraps:

Wraps:
Wraps:
Wraps:
Wraps:
Wraps:
Wraps:
Wraps:
Wraps:

Wraps:
Cloth:
Wraps:
Wraps:
Wraps:
Cloth:
Wraps:
Wraps:
Cloth:
Wraps:
Cloth:
Wraps:
Wraps:
Wraps:
Wraps:
Wraps:
Cloth:
Wraps:
Wraps:
Wraps:
Ltd:

Wraps:
Wraps:
Wraps:
Ltd:
Wraps:
Wraps:
Wraps:
Wraps:
Wraps:
Wraps:
Wraps:
Cloth:
Wraps:
Wraps:
Wraps:
Cloth:
Wraps:
Wraps:
Cloth:

Wraps:
Ltd:
Folder:
Wraps:
Ltd:

Wraps:
Ltd:
Tape:
Wraps:
Ltd:
Wraps:
Ltd:
Wraps:
Ltd:
Tape:

Wraps:
Ltd:
Wraps:
Cloth:
Ltd:
Wraps:
Ltd:
Wraps:
Cloth:
Ltd:
Wraps:
Cloth:
Ltd:

Wraps:
Cloth:
Ltd:
Wraps:
Wraps:
Ltd:
Wraps:
Ltd:
Wraps:
Cloth:
Ltd:
Wraps:
Ltd:
Wraps:
Ltd:
Wraps:
Ltd:
Cloth:
Ltd:
Wraps:
Ltd:
Cloth:
Ltd:
Wraps:
Cloth:
Ltd:

Wraps:
Wraps:
Wraps:
Wraps:
Wraps:

Wraps:
Wraps:
Ltd:
Wraps:
Ltd:
Tape:
Wraps:
Ltd:
Wraps:
Tape:
Wraps:
Ltd:
Wraps:
Ltd:
Wraps:
Foreign:
Tape:
Wraps:
Wraps:
Ltd:
Wraps:
Ltd:
Wraps:
Foreign:
Tape:

Wraps:
Wraps:
Broadside:
Wraps:
Wraps:
Wraps:
Wraps:
Wraps:
Wraps:
Wraps:
Wraps:
Wraps:
Wraps:
Wraps:
Wraps:

Answers: A-7, B-3, C-9, D-6, E-10, F-13, G-8, H-12, I-1, J-11, K-4, L-5, M-2.

Answers: a-2, b-7, c-10, d-8, e-9, f-1, g-4, h-6, i-3, j-5.

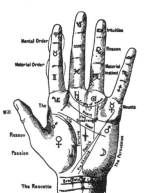

Maybe
You Will
And Maybe
You Won't

...continue
IT DEPENDS

Name _____

Address _____

_____

Self   Spouse
○   ○
○   ○

"...The bloated Cadaver of poor Mrs. Hays."

Phewww!

SOLID TRIANGLES—

◄ ►   ◄ ►   ◄ ►   ◄ ►   ◄ ►

DOOR CLOSER

JAMB CLOSER BRACKET

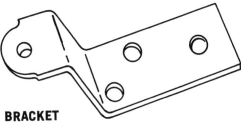

CLOSER JAMB BRACKET

DOOR CLOSER BRACKET

17...

34...

51...shift
or latch!

say goodbye

Annual bluegrass	Foxtail
Barnyard grass	Goosegrass
Browntop panicum	Lovegrass
Carpetweed	Purslane
Chickweed	Spurge
Crabgrass	Stinkgrass
Fall panicum	Texas millet.
Florida pussley	Witchgrass

Bindweed	Nettle
Bitterweed	Pennycress
Broomweed	Pennywort
Carpetweed	Peppergrass
Chickweed	Plantain
Chicory	Poor Jo
Croton	Puncture Vine
Dandelion	Ragweed
Dock	Shepherd's Purse
Fan Weed	Spurge
Knotweed	Thistle
Kochia	Wild Carrot
Mallows	Wild Lettuce
Morning Glory	Yarrow
Mustard . . . and many, many other	

Sclerotinia dollar spot
Rhizoctonia brown patch
Piricularia gray leaf spot
Curvularia and Helminthosporium
leaf spot
Blights—
Going out
Fading out
Melting out

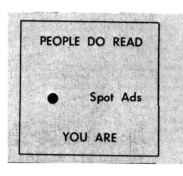

THE MARKETING MAZE

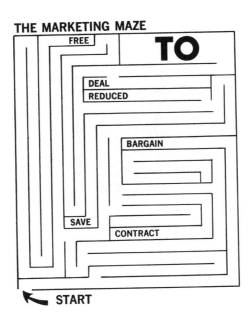

FREE

TO

DEAL
REDUCED

BARGAIN

SAVE
CONTRACT

START

LONESOME
?
Call
536-6091

F . . . Friendship

R . . . Rob

I . . . Involvement?
irrevocable.

E . . . Exciting, expensive, enticing, exotic, exorbitant, exulting, extrava-
gant . . . and with just a touch of . . . Eternity. It's

N . . . Notably neurotic, narcotic, a nuisance, a Nymph

D . . . Dame . . . as in Grande

S . . . Self. That which must be added

H . . . Happy and harrassed hours, harranges with holes, hoops, and
hawsers . . .

I . . . Interested?

P . . . Patience; you'll get one

you can't afford new

you can't afford to
you can't afford to
you can't afford to
you can't afford to
you can't afford to
you can't afford to
you can't afford to
you can't afford to
you can't afford to
you can't afford to

you can't afford new

History of Sex
Dimensions of Sex
Philosophy of Sex
You and Sex
Male and Female Sex
Art of Sex
Positions for Sex
Female Oral-Anal Sex
Male Oral-Anal Sex
Female Techniques for Sex
Male Techniques for Sex
Menstration Sex
Pregnancy Sex
Substitute Sex
Satisfying Sex
Old Sex
Ill Sex
Handicapped Sex
Compiled Sex
Handbook Sex
Sex

BOWWOWWOWOHGODOHMAN
IWANNADIEBOWWOWWOW

TABLE VII

the Manipulations of

Member	Navami 9th day	Chaturdashi 14th day	Purnima Full Moon	Amavasya New Moon
Yoni	Thrust violently with Linga or even rub hard with hand	Scratch, press in member till her waist bends	"	Manipulate and pull open like a flower
Navel	Rub and frequently pass hand over	"	"	"
Lip	Kiss and suck	"	Kiss in various ways[1]	Kiss in various ways
Side	Press with fingers & scratch very softly	"	"	"
Breast	Rub, squeeze twist, & make it very small	"	Pull hard	Scratch till it bears nail-marks
Chest	"	"	Scratch and leave marks	Scratch and leave marks
Nipple	"	"	Kiss and rub with thumb and forefinger	Pass hand over it and rub with thumb and forefinger
Body generally	"	"	Embrace in various ways	Embrace in various ways and press
Eye	"	Kiss	Kiss	Kiss
Armpit	"	"	Scratch and tickle	Scratch and tickle

 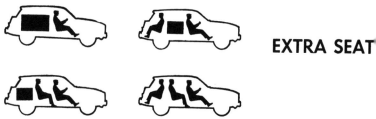

EXTRA SEAT

Univers c omposit ion sizes are on th e monot ype and t

he Univers matching display si zes are on the Monotype too!

Coffee, pillow, magazine, snack, refreshments, baby's bottle, question, dinner for 130, jetcetera, jetcetera...

xxxxxxxxxxxxxxxxxxxxx

THE

NEW

HOT

PANTS

LOOK

xxxxxxxxxxxxxxxxxxxxx

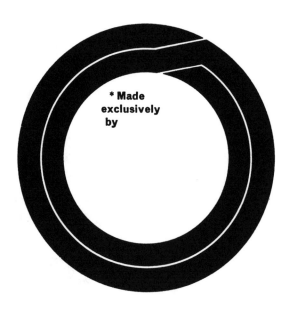

* Made
exclusively
by

I have since.

VII

I think I have discovered something very important, but I am not yet sure what it is.

The other night I had some tapioca pudding and I began eating it, and I said *nnnnuuuuunnnggguuunnnnggg-uuuunnnngggg* to myself. It seemed to enhance the taste. I'm sure of that. But perhaps I wanted it to, for Felix's sake.

Six hundred lines of blank verse without any bumble-bees or sunsets is a pretty stiff dose.

INPUT POWER

OUTPUT

TRANSDUCER
EXCITATION

FREQUENCY

GAIN

GAIN STABILITY

FREQUENCY
RESPONSE

NON-LINEARITY

INPUT IMPEDANCE

OUTPUT IMPEDANCE

OUTPUT RIPPLE

LOAD IMPEDANCE

BALANCE
ADJUST RANGE

ZERO SHIFT

DRIFT

ISOLATION

WEIGHT

CASE

CONSTRUCTION

IDENTIFICATION

ALTITUDE

TEMPERATURE

VIBRATION

ACCELERATION

SHOCK

ATMOSPHERE

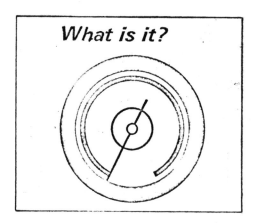

own your own

CLEAN—AIR BENCH

CLEAN-ROOM CLOTHING

MECHANICAL FLOOR MATS

6 switches
are
5 more
than you

boil
deli
mbl

$$\frac{\int o^r [M - \frac{u}{l}] a}{C^{om}_{p} o\text{-}s^i t \left(\frac{io}{n}\right)}$$

HIGHEST   **GREATEST**   **LOWEST**

Exercise J
1. -ance
2. -ish
3. -ant
4. -ity
5. -ive
6. -ment
7. -y
8. -ness
9. -less
10. -ion
11. -ance
12. -ion
13. -al
14. -ation
15. -ly
16. -ness

-ness as in happiness
-ment as in statement
-ence as in difference
-ance as in assistance
-ation as in foundation
-ion as in action
-ity as in activity

How do you do?
My name is, or I'm . . . .
What's your name?
I'm from the U.S. (England, France, Canada,
        Soviet Union)
Where do you live?
I'm a business man.
    " teacher.
    " secretary.
    " doctor.
    " college professor.
    " student.
    " housewife.
    " engineer.
    " bum.
How about a cup of coffee?
    "   a cup of tea?
    "   a drink?

Tizz
Tizz
Tizz and
Tizz at
Tizz at
Tizz in
Tizz in
Tizz in
Tizz is a
Tizz on a
Tizz on a
Tizz on a
Tizz Plays
Tizz Takes

the number.

EXAMPLE: No. B26694

Cal
g
g
mg
mg
I.U.
mg
mg
mg

-PLAY:

                      : jiggle, pinch, shake, squeeze . . .
see oral arts.

: pat, rub, pinch, scratch, enbosom . . .
      see oral arts.

: press, rub, up-down digitation, scratch, enbreast . . .
      see oral arts.

      : same as
    see oral arts.

sincere souffles?
opulent omelets?
crazy casseroles?
rambunctious ragouts?
precocious pastas?
ambitious aspics?
devastating desserts?
loony legumes?
enchanting enchiladas?
bewitching breads?

do mad, marvelous things with food.

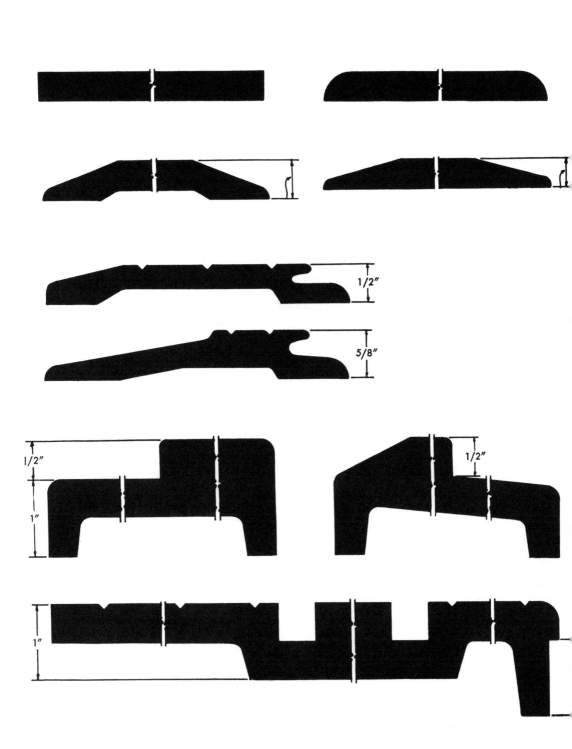

—(count them!):
The governor of North Carolina.
The governor of South Carolina.
The governor of Tennessee.
The governor of Arkansas.
The governor of Virginia.
The governor of Kentucky.
The governor of Texas.
The governor of Florida.
ONLY the governor of Louisiana

10
to ask
before

1. Can I get good
2. Will the people have natural facial color?
           No green faces?
3. Will the background
            No blue grass?
4. How easy
5. Does it come
6. What

7. Who
8. Suppose
9. Can I
10. Can I

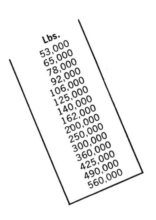

Lbs.
53,000
65,000
78,000
92,000
106,000
125,000
140,000
162,000
200,000
250,000
300,000
360,000
425,000
490,000
560,000

four kinds

1. Love acquired by continual habit.
2. Love resulting from the imagination.
3. Love resulting from belief.
4. Love resulting from the perception of external objects.

FORGET...
The TRAINING
The DISCIPLINE
The EXPERIENCE
The LEADERSHIP
The TEAMWORK
The SKILLS
The PERSISTENCE

 MOLY

GEAR-MOLY

MOLY-SEAL

TWO-CYCLE MOLY

New <u>AUTO-MOLY</u>
DOUBLE

 **AUTO-MOLY**

TOPOIL-MOLY

HANDI-MOLY

The naked truth!

10. It explains how to

18. It shows you

11. It reveals how a

19. It gives you

12. It shows you the

20. It explains how

13. It tells you how to get

21. It reveals how

14. It tells how to avoid

22. It explains how

15. It shows you how to turn

23. It shows you how

16. It explains how to get your

24. It gives you

17. It tells you how to

25. It shows how

Types

Excellent	Good	Poor
Excellent	Good	Fair
Excellent	Good	Poor
Poor	Excellent	Probably excellent
Good	Excellent	Poor
Excellent	Good	Poor
Fair-excellent	Excellent-poor	Probably excellent
Fair	?	Probably excellent
Excellent	Poor High	Probably good
Moderate-low		Probably low (eventually)

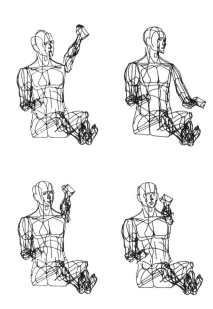

```
goodk kkkkk unjam ingwe nches lass? start again goodk
lassw enche sking start again kings tart! again sorry
goodk ingwe ncesl ooked outas thef? unmix asloo kedou
tonth effff rewri tenow goodk ingwe ncesl asloo kedou
tonth effff fffff unjam feast ofsai ntste venst efanc
utsai ntrew ritef easto fstep toeso rryan dsons orry!
start again good? yesgo odkin gwenc eslas looke dout?
doubt wrong track start again goodk ingwe ncesl asloo
kedou tonth efeas tofst ephph phphp hphph unjam phphp
repea tunja mhphp scrub carol hphph repea tscru bcaro
lstop subst itute track merry chris tmasa ndgoo dnewy
earin 1699? check digit banks orryi n1966 endme ssage
```

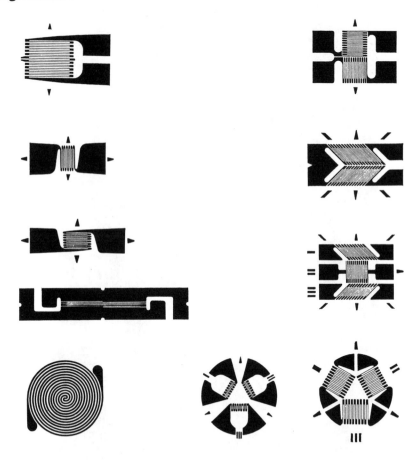

	Yes	Undecided	No
	☐	☐	☐
	☐	☐	☐
	☐	☐	☐
	☐	☐	☐
	☐	☐	☐
	☐	☐	☐
	☐	☐	☐

....
....
....

....
....
....

ROY C. HANNUM, W. JACK YOUNG,
LEWIS G. SMITH, ROBERT D. OLSEN,
PHILIP F. SCHAMBERGER, JR.
HAROLD L. CREAMER, PAUL R. HAU,
CARL P. HETZEL, MILTON F. HILL,
CHARLES BRUNELL, JOHN R. POST,
RICHARD L. GROBEN, FRED SAUER,
ROBERT W. JOHNSON, KENNETH
W. TWIGG, MARSHALL A. PEEPLES,
HERBERT DREISBACH, JR., JOHN
J. GEMINDER, JOSEPH CROBAK,

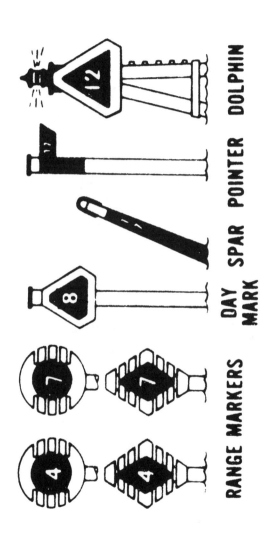

RANGE MARKERS · DAY MARK · SPAR · POINTER · DOLPHIN

	1ST YEAR	2ND YEAR	3RD YEAR	4TH YEAR	TOTALS
	(top 1, left 0, right 1, bottom 1)	(top 1, left 0, right 1, bottom 2)	(top 1, left 1, right 1, bottom 1)	(top 1, left 1, right 1, bottom 1)	(top 4, left 2, right 4, bottom 5)
	(top 0, left 0, right 0, bottom 0)	(top 0, left 0, right 0, bottom 1)	(top 1, left 0, right 1, bottom 1)	(top 1, left 1, right 0, bottom 1)	(top 2, left 1, right 1, bottom 3)
	(top 1, left 0, right 1, bottom 1)	(top 1, left 0, right 1, bottom 1)	(top 1, left 1, right 1, bottom 2)	(top 1, left 1, right 1, bottom 1)	(top 4, left 2, right 4, bottom 5)
	(top 1, left 0, right 1, bottom 1)	(top 2, left 1, right 1, bottom 1)	(top 2, left 1, right 0, bottom 2)	(top 3, left 0, right 1, bottom 2)	(top 8, left 2, right 3, bottom 6)
	(top 0, left 0, right 1, bottom 0)	(top 1, left 0, right 1, bottom 2)	(top 2, left 2, right 3, bottom 2)	(top 1, left 2, right 3, bottom 3)	(top 4, left 4, right 8, bottom 7)
	(top 3, left 0, right 4, bottom 3)	(top 5, left 1, right 4, bottom 7)	(top 7, left 5, right 6, bottom 8)	(top 7, left 5, right 6, bottom 8)	(top 22, left 11, right 20, bottom 26)

END NO MO
CLOSED

THE eND

THE END

8569   8332   7876   8678

AFTERWORD

BY MARK MELNICOVE

THE LAST ACTS OF BERN PORTER
FEBRUARY 14, 1911 TO JUNE 7, 2004

THE ABNEGATING OF NEGATING

THE BEAUTIFICATION OF RUDIMENTATION

THE CONDENSATION OF EXULTATION

THE DEIFICATION OF DECAY

THE EMBOUNDING OF FOUNDS

THE FINGERING OF LINGERING

THE GRAVITAS OF RAVE

THE HYPERSPACING OF ERASING

THE IMPROVISING OF IMPROVING

THE JUSTIFICATION OF IF

THE KILLING OF NIL

THE LEVITY OF INEVITABILITY

THE MERGING OF ERGS

THE NEFARIOUSNESS OF FAR

THE OBSOLESCENCE OF OBSOLESCENCE

THE PERSONIFICATION OF HIMSELF

THE QUIESCENCE OF ESSENCE

THE RAPTURE OF ORDURE

THE SEXING OF NEXTING

THE TOUGHNESS OF ENOUGHNESS

THE UPKEEP OF WEEP

THE VIRTUE OF TRUE

THE WRATH OF THAT

THE X-ING OF KVETCHING

THE YESSING OF JESTING

THE ZEROING OF INFINITY

BERN PORTER
CONCURS

Left: Bern Porter, print by Enid Foster, 1946. George J. Mitchell Department of Special Collections & Archives, Bowdoin College, Brunswick, Maine, Bern Porter Collection.

A Humanity is slowly evolving into a higher intelligence but under tremendous resistance and negative forces. The pulsating, expanding, contracting vibrant energy plasma which I call intelligence, sends, receives, assimilates, manages and controls energy data bits within the confines of a present five-sense system. Breakthroughs beyond these five were obviously intended in the original neural concept but to this date have been hamstrung and left bruised, even damaged, by prevailing political, economic, social, educational and environmental factors.

It is possible, if we could get free of polluted food, polluted air and water, and we could get free of the drugs and chemicals, that we could purify ourselves and go on to these extra levels.

B All I try to do is feel the Founds visually and sensuously; I don't rationalize them.

C I use poetic principles to study nature. According to me, a poet and a scientist are one and the same thing. What a theoretical physicist goes through is no different than what a poet goes through.

Perhaps to clarify that poetry has changed I should now list the types by name which have engrossed me here in Maine these past sixty years, types apart from jingles, free verse, greeting card rimes, sonnets, Homerics, Elizabethan, Shakespearian, Romantic and Classical forms everyone knows (and which I have also produced in my time):

Concrete Visual Poems	Lettrism Poetry	Poetry-Language
Concrete Poems	Genre Painting Poems	Visual Poetry
Found Visual Poetry	Urban Poems	Sound Poetry
Behaviorist Poetry	Objective Poetry	Experimental Poetry
Conceptual Poetry	Poesia Visiva	Baroque Form Poems
Landscape Poems	Polemical Poetry	Baroque Church Poetry
Phonism Poetry	Politicized Poetry	Found Poetry
Hermetical Poetry	Action Poetry	Gesture Poetry
Graphic Poetry	Poetry of Permutation	Wall Poetry
Typographical Poetry	Do-It-Yourself Poetry	Poetry of Nothing
Dimensional Poetry	Attitude Poetry	
Spatial Poetry	Body Poetry	

D The truth is that when World War II was over, atomic power was sold for a dollar to GE and a dollar to Westinghouse, and they just ran with it so fast they never bothered to figure what to do with the waste, what to do with leakage, what to do about human errors. I'm afraid that now it is an uncontrollable monster.

E In school I always read aloud the word 'nowhere' as 'now here'.

F Others say I'm running the found cut-out deal into the ground; also stealing other people's stuff. Personally, I'm still looking for what I'm looking for.

G Physicists are probably the most religious people in the world. My community is with nature. I just look out the window and that's all I need. It is incredible.

H My boredom increased until I tore volumes from library shelves, dipped them one by one in a secret solution which cleared the printed words cleanly from every page. These words floated freely atop the bluish liquid forming a darksome sludge which I skimmed off with a wooden ladle. With an insoluble, erasable ink I daubed each newly pristine page of every treated volume, 'You Too'.

I I don't just want to be ironic, satirical, in an age of irony. Underneath the Founds and through their juxtaposition, I want there to be a sense of the traditional and the modern values for which I've always fought.

J During the few precious moments of relaxation, some of us roamed the Tennessee ridges speaking tiredly yet confidently of tremendous contributions to mankind—new freedoms from disease and the like.

K Here we are blasting into space, and we still haven't figured out what we have here.

L Sure I'm mixed up, but no more than anybody else in these days.

M Undoubtedly the same cars that passed us as we turned from the main highway to find the illusive gorge now sped by us a second time on that bright fall day. They, too, had gone nowhere and were now returning.

N NEVER A MIDDLEMAN!

O Obsolescence revolts me. The alleged modern is a repetition of the ancient decorated in chrome, styled with air-flow and color-engineered to abomination.

P It was the revolting, nauseous and wholly unbearable nature of obsolescence itself that drove me to more concerted concentration of the inherent possibilities within and finally to a point where I pressed the membrane separating man and God closer and closer to the Ultimate and indeed felt occasions when I had pierced the barrier sufficiently to more than look past. The first to raise himself by his own boot-straps I was thus able to see, hear, taste, feel and smell all things at all times. Through the combined use of these faculties I became all things at any time in any place. Thus endowed, being so, I became me.

Q
SING THAT MEAT
MEET THAT SONG
SING THE BEAT
BEAT THOSE NOTES
VOICE THE ESSENCE
BLOW THE THING
PUSH IT HIGH
WIDE
DEEP
AND HANDSOME
Oh My Brother
SING

R Nuggets of value in the waste are everywhere for the looking, if only the viewer can develop his or her wisdom of the questioning eye.

S Then, too, there was an oxen's yoke hanging on a peg that recalled the stories Gram used to tell how Great Grandsire drove his team of oxen over the Aroostook Road to Bangor, to get molasses for his bride.

T If the scientists had the guts of longshoremen who go out on strike for their 10 cent increase, they would all refuse to work on weapons of destruction.

U I believe that I am guilty. [Voice breaks, tears in his eyes.] I'm sorry...that I...even at this late date...I'm sorry that I ever had anything to do with the atomic bomb...sorry that I used my talent...I spent ten years [1945-1955] wandering the Pacific in a fog, not knowing who I was or what I wanted to do or why I was guilty, and ashamed and sorry I was a physicist.

V In an old Scottish tenet it is said that 'the purpose of life is to praise God and enjoy His creation.' One cannot perform these functions without first setting his inner house in order, making gifts to his enemies and converting kindly thoughts and words to deeds of equal friendless for all with whom he comes in contact. So released, the blessings one receives are beyond measure.

W When you are dealing with waste, how do you avoid using crude material? So, you have to find the artistic value in crude.

X Confronting the bombed buildings, the concentration camps and the gulags, artists had the choice of saying nothing or transforming anything that came to hand into something new.

Y Later, in a surge of creative intensity, a kind of coma wherein there is no hesitation, no uncertainty, no forced thinking, no rational control; a state of relaxed abandonment in which one seems to know without knowing, a psychological state to which one ascends while leaving body, mind, and senses behind, I instantly and in one operation turned the seascape horizontally, clipped it into a body form with shore, hill, and wave lines automatically becoming, as I clipped, the folds and forms of a clownlike suit, placed it under the headform at the upper right and knew the process was for me aesthetically final.

Z I finger zero, readjust my couch in a void that sloth built, the better to do nothing.

Bern Porter's Strobe-Disk, from BERN PORTER: TO THE WORLD, Roger Jackson,
Publisher, 1999. Belfast Free Library, Belfast, Maine, Bern Porter Collection.

SOURCES

A. Melnicove, Mark, ed., *Sounds That Arouse Me: Selected Writings*, Tilbury House, Publishers, 1992, p. 131; Dunbar, Margaret, ed., Bern! Porter! Interview!, The Dog Ear Press, 1981, p. 47.

B. Schevill, James, *Where to Go, What to Do, When You Are Bern Porter: A Personal Biography*, Tilbury House, Publishers, 1992, p. 308.

C. Kramer, Barbara, "Bern Porter: Artist, Scientist and Poet," *Preview!*, August 2-9, 1991, p. 9; Porter, Bern, "Morsels from Daily Life, in George Myers, Jr., ed., *Alphabets Sublime: Contemporary Artists on Collage and Visual Literature*, Paycock Press, 1986.

D. Kramer, Ibid, p. 9.

E. Porter, Bern, "A Yankee Visits The Tavern Here," New Hampshire Gazette, April 2, 1937.

F. Schevill, op.cit., p. 314.

G. Mayers, Art, "Bern Porter at 80: Still Doing It His Way," *Maine Progressive*, May 1991, page 27.

H. Porter, Bern, *I've Left: a manifesto and a testament of science and art*, Something Else Press, 1971, p. ?

I. Schevill, op.cit., p. 308.

J. Stone, Judy, "Former Atomic Scientist Now Promotes Experimental Art," *Independent Journal*, April 8, 1950, p. M10.

K. Goodyear, Sarah, "Artful Codger," *Down East*, October 1993, p. 81.

L. Stone, op.cit., p. M10.

M. Porter, "A Yankee Visits The Tavern Here," op.cit.

N. Porter, Bern, *Here Comes Everybody's Don't Book*, The Dog Ear Press, 1984, last page.

O. Porter, *I've Left*, op. cit., p. 1.

P. Ibid, p. 11.

Q. Melnicove, *Sounds That Arouse Me*, op.cit., p. 33.

R. Schevill, op.cit., p. 297.

S. Porter, "A Yankee Visits The Tavern Here," op.cit.

T. Stone, op.cit., p. M10.

U. *Observations from the Treadmill*, Union, ME, 1975, p. 6.

V. Stone, op.cit., p. M10.

W. Schevill, op.cit., p. 300.

X. Schevill, Ibid., p. 295.

Y. Schevill, Ibid., p. 101.

Z. Porter, *I've Left*, op. cit., p. 1.

Right: "Five Women," Found Photo Collage by Bern Porter and Mark Melnicove, 2010. Mark Melnicove Collection.

B14 $24.95

NIGHTBOAT BOOKS

Nightboat Books, a nonprofit organization, seeks to develop
audiences for writers whose work resists convention and
transcends boundaries. We publish book rich with poignancy,
intelligence, and risk. Please visit our website, www.nightboat.
org, to learn about our titles and how you can support our
future publications.

The following individuals have supported the publication
of this book. We thank them for their generosity and
commitment to the mission of Nigahtboat Books:

Kazim Ali
Photios Giovanis
Sarah Heller
Tod Lippy
Elizabeth Motika
Benjamin Taylor

In addition, this book has been made possible, in part, by a
grant from the New York State Council on the Arts Literature
Program.

State of the Arts

NYSCA